PARIS-CONNECTION

THE ASSASSINATION OF PRINCESS DIANA

JOHN MORGAN

First published in Australia by Shining Bright Publishing
Printed by Lightning Source

ISBN: 978-0-9807407-5-2

Paris-London Connection

Is dedicated

To

Diana, Princess of Wales

And

Dodi Fayed

Killed in a mindless tragedy

The crash in the Alma Tunnel, Paris, at 12.23 a.m., 31 August 1997

And

To those few in their and Henri Paul's families

Who have had the courage to fight for the truth to come out

Who have been confronted with an unconscionable
travesty of justice

Known as the official investigations

That commenced in Paris immediately after the crash

That concluded at 4.33 p.m. on 7 April 2008 in London's
Royal Courts of Justice

The information in this book is based on over 5,000 pages of evidence within the *Diana Inquest* book series:

Part 1: Diana Inquest: **The Untold Story** (2009)

Covers pre-crash events in the Ritz Hotel, the final journey and what happened in the Alma Tunnel

Part 2: Diana Inquest: **How & Why Did Diana Die?** (2009)

Covers possible motives for assassination and post-crash medical treatment of Princess Diana – including deliberate mistreatment in the ambulance

Part 3: Diana Inquest: **The French Cover-Up** (2010)

Covers the fraudulent autopsies of the driver, Henri Paul, and the misconduct of the French investigation into the crash

Part 4: Diana Inquest: **The British Cover-Up** (2011)

Covers the post-death treatment of Princess Diana – including the embalmings and autopsies carried out in both France and the UK and the post-crash cover-up by UK authorities, including the Queen

Part 5: Diana Inquest: **Who Killed Princess Diana?** (2012)

Covers the involvement of MI6 and senior British royals in the assassinations of Princess Diana and Dodi Fayed

Diana Inquest: **The Documents the Jury Never Saw** (2010)

Reproduces hundreds of key documents from within the British Operation Paget investigation – all documents that the inquest jury were prevented from seeing

Table of Contents

Read This First

This is a short work, but don't be deceived!

Paris-London Connection is the product of six years of full-time forensic research. It is based on the official Paget report, inquest transcripts and hundreds of police documents – all related to the 1997 Paris crash that resulted in the deaths of Princess Diana, Dodi Fayed and Henri Paul.

This research led to the compilation of the *Diana Inquest* series of books – detailed volumes that have addressed each major aspect of the case. (A list appears at the front of this book).

Without those volumes, this condensed, evidence-based narrative you hold in your hand could not have been written.

Acknowledgements

During the years of research I have received invaluable support from various individuals.

No acknowledgements could start with anyone other than my wife, Lana – she has been a huge rock of strength amidst the madness of constant writing and progressing illness.

Lana – who identifies herself as the devil's advocate – has contributed immensely as a regular sounding board for ideas and analysis and has provided invaluable input into concepts and opinion during the development of the *Diana Inquest* volumes.

On top of that, Lana has acted as artistic director with the principal role of designing the cover for each volume. She has also assisted with editing, thoroughly reading and re-reading manuscripts prior to publication.

Without Lana's support the volumes – and therefore this book – could never have been produced.

Paul Sparks, UK-based journalist and film producer, has been an extremely consistent support right from the earliest beginnings of this series. Paul has provided invaluable help in filling the inevitable geographical void that is created as a result of the books being written in Australia – thousands of kilometres away from where the key events occurred.

I also am indebted to a forensic investigator in London, who commenced assembling an extensive archive with case notes on the Paris crash and its aftermath, within a week of the tragedy occurring. This person has constantly maintained and updated their records over the ensuing 15 years and has kindly passed on research information from that archive whenever I have requested it. They wish to remain anonymous.

As well, it should be evident to any reader of the volumes that the hundreds of documents from within the MPS Paget investigation that were passed onto me a few years ago have been a huge help in completing a thorough investigation of the crash and the resulting cover-up. I am very grateful to the people in the UK who threw caution to the wind and courageously provided me with that invaluable information. Without those documents virtually none of Part 4 could have been written. So, although the documents the jury never saw have lengthened this investigative project, it has more importantly filled in critical gaps in the jigsaw that would otherwise have been impossible to fit.

There are other people in the UK who have assisted in sometimes critical ways, but wish or need to remain anonymous. To those people, who know who they are, I am extremely thankful for their assistance and they can hopefully appreciate that they have contributed towards establishing the historical record of what occurred in certainly one of the most significant assassinations of our time.

Then there are more individuals – all living outside of the UK – who have assisted in various ways and I wish to gratefully acknowledge their support: Jayne Dean, Emmanuelle Quignon, Monica Hudson, Margaret Deters, Jos Deters, Rex Morgan and Sue Hindle and Simone Mackinnon.

In specific reference to the knowledge now available regarding the activities of MI6, I wish to acknowledge the uncompromising courage of the late Peter Wright[1], Richard Tomlinson, David Shayler and Annie Machon. They have all been prepared to go public to address important issues that would otherwise have remained officially buried and hidden from our collective understanding.

---

[1] Peter Wright died in Australia in 1995, aged 78.

Preface

This is the story of an event that shocked the world.

At 12.23 a.m. on Sunday 31 August 1997 a Mercedes S280 limousine carrying Diana, Princess of Wales and her lover, Dodi Fayed, careered at 60 mph into the 13th pillar of Paris' Alma Tunnel.

Paris-London Connection relates the events that led up to and precipitated that historic crash and the inter-governmental cover-up of information that followed it.

In doing that, this book answers many of the questions that have been left unanswered by the three official investigations into the circumstances of the Alma crash.

The information included in this short book is drawn from the six published – and one yet to be published – volumes of the *Diana Inquest* series of books, listed earlier. Any reader who is looking for the evidence to back up what is written here should go to those volumes – they include over 5,000 pages of witness and documentary evidence accompanied by a thorough forensic analysis.

Not every aspect or detail of the case is covered in this book. It has instead been compiled as an easy-to-read narrative, showing the major events that took place. To that end, and to assist with story flow and readability, footnotes and endnotes have been mostly omitted – but there is a thorough Bibliography included.

The assassination of Princess Diana was a joint intelligence operation – including British MI6, French DGSE and the US CIA.

Only with access to individual phone or banking records would it be possible to know which agencies each agent was working directly for. So to simplify the flow of the book it has generally been addressed throughout as an MI6 operation. It is certainly MI6 that received the initial order to carry out the assassination and it was conducted under the MI6 umbrella.

For example, Henri Paul has been named in the book as an MI6 agent, but it is possible he had been recruited by French agencies DST or DGSE. Ultimately he was working in an MI6 operation, even though his intelligence handler could have been French.

Word Usage:

"Autopsy" and "post-mortem" are synonymous – "autopsy" is generally used in France, whereas "post-mortem" is generally used in the UK

KP = Kensington Palace, Diana's home

Sapeurs Pompiers = Paris Fire Service

BAC = Blood Alcohol Concentration

"Cours la Reine", "Cours Albert 1er", "Avenue de New York" and "Voie Georges Pompidou" are all names for the same riverside expressway that runs into the Alma Tunnel. The parallel service road is also known as "Cours Albert 1er"

Fulham Mortuary = Hammersmith and Fulham Mortuary

Imperial College = Charing Cross Hospital

MI6 = SIS = Secret Intelligence Service

MI5 = SS = Security Service

Abbreviations

BAC = Blood Alcohol Concentration
BCA = Bureau Central des Accidents
BJL = Bernard J. Lane
CDT = Carbohydrate-Deficient Transferrin
CIA = Central Intelligence Agency
DGSE = Direction Générale de la Securité
DST = Directorate de Surveillance Territories
ENB = English National Ballet
IML = L'Institut Médico-Legal de Paris
LCO = Lord Chamberlain's Office
LGC = Laboratory of the Government Chemist
MPS = Metropolitan Police Service
NSA = National Security Agency
OCG = Organised Crime Group
PFG = Pompes Funèbres Générales
SAMU = Service d'Aide Médicale d'Urgence
SAS = Special Air Service
SIO = Senior Investigating Officer
WAG = Way Ahead Group

PARIS-LONDON CONNECTION

Timeline

1989

Dec 31   Private (Squidgygate) conversation between Diana and her friend, James Gilbey, is secretly recorded

1990

Jan 4   Diana-Gilbey conversation recording is rebroadcast and this is picked up by two individual private ham operators, Cyril Reenan and Jean Norman, acting separately

1991

Mar   Journalist, Andrew Morton, writes an article in the *Sunday Times*, based on deliberately leaked information from Princess Diana, regarding the situation in the Charles-Diana household

Apr   Diana and Brazilian ambassador's wife, Lucia Flecha de Lima, travel to Brazil with their husbands – this is the beginning of the Diana-Lucia friendship

Jul   Diana's friend, James Colthurst, starts conducting interviews with her on behalf of Andrew Morton at Kensington Palace

Nov   Andrew Morton's central London office is burgled – his files are gone through, and a camera stolen

Dec   Patrick Jephson, Diana's private secretary, warns Diana that the "men in grey suits" know about the Morton book and her involvement in it

1992

Jan   Diana is warned by Buckingham Palace that they are aware of her co-operation with Morton's book

Feb   Rosa Monckton's initial meeting with Diana

Jun	
7	Serialisation of *Diana: Her True Story* begins in the *Sunday Times*
15	Publication of Andrew Morton book *Diana: Her True Story*
18	Philip sends first letter to Diana
Aug 24	*The Sun* publishes the Squidgygate transcripts
Nov	Royal Way Ahead Group is set up and holds first meeting
24	Queen declares 1992 as her "annus horribilus" at the City of London's Guildhall
25	Charles requests a formal separation at Kensington Palace. Diana agrees to it
27	Announcement that Queen is prepared to start paying tax
Dec 9	Prime Minister John Major announces the separation in Parliament

1993

Aug	Holiday with Diana, Rosa, Lucia and Beatriz (Lucia's daughter) at Bali and Moyo Island, Indonesia – organised by Rosa

1995

Oct	Diana passes handwritten note to her butler, Paul Burrell, stating that Charles is planning a staged car crash
30	Meeting between Diana and her lawyer, Victor Mishcon – Diana says she fears a staged car crash
Nov	Brakes fail while Diana is driving her Audi
20	BBC *Panorama* broadcasts Diana interview by Martin Bashir
Dec	
10	Queen consults with Prime Minister John Major and the Archbishop of Canterbury about a potential Charles-Diana divorce
11	*Time* magazine quotes a "veteran royal watcher": "The Queen is disgusted with [Diana] and wishes she'd just go away"

18	Diana receives a handwritten letter from the Queen, requesting her to divorce Charles
19	Diana receives a letter from Charles, requesting a divorce

1996

Jul	Diana commences involvement in the anti-landmine campaign
Aug 28	Divorce between Charles and Diana becomes final
Sep 16	Way Ahead Group (WAG) meeting held

1997

Jan	
12	Diana starts anti-landmine trip to Angola
16	Diana's Angolan anti-landmine trip finishes
20	WAG meeting held
Feb	Diana is warned to drop her anti-landmine campaign and is threatened with an "accident"
May	
1	Tony Blair's Labour Party sweeps to power in the UK
21	UK announces ban on the import, export, transfer and manufacture of landmines
Jun	Diana provides Simone Simmons with a copy of her "Profiting out of Misery " dossier
1	Rosa Monckton's daughter, Domenica Lawson's, 2nd birthday
3	Royal gala performance of Swan Lake at the Royal Albert Hall – Mohamed Al Fayed invites Diana to holiday at his St Tropez residence
11	Diana writes note to Mohamed saying she and the boys are "greatly looking forward to" the St Tropez holiday
12	Diana makes major anti-landmine address to Royal Geographic Society stating that she is on a personal anti-landmine crusade

13	Camilla Parker-Bowles, Charles' mistress, suffers a minor injury resulting from a serious car crash in Wiltshire
25	Diana is forced to withdraw from attending a Landmines Eradication Group meeting in parliament
30	Rosa Monckton arranges to borrow a boat from "friends" to use on a Greek Island holiday cruise with Diana set for mid-August

Jul

6	Diana's final meeting with Prime Minister Tony Blair at Chequers
8	Preparatory meeting for July 23 WAG meeting
9	David Davies phones Robert Fellowes, the Queen's private secretary, warning of police concerns about Diana's upcoming holiday to St Tropez
11	Diana, William and Harry travel to St Tropez for a 10 day holiday with the Al Fayed family
14	Dodi Fayed joins the group in St Tropez
18	Camilla's 50th birthday party is held at Highgrove
20	Diana, William and Harry return to London from St Tropez
	Mirror article states that "Diana" is top of the agenda at the next WAG meeting
21 to 23	Diana and Dodi share significant periods of time together, including visits to Dodi's apartment and a private movie viewing
23	WAG meeting held
24	Diana visits her sister Sarah and stays for 2 nights
26	Diana visits Paris with Dodi
27	Diana and Dodi return to London
29	Diana meets with boyfriend, Hasnat Khan, in Battersea Park
30	Diana breaks off her relationship with Hasnat at Kensington Palace
31	Diana travels with Dodi to Nice and they board the *Jonikal* commencing a 7 day holiday, cruising the French and Italian Mediterranean

TIMELINE

Aug

5   Diana and Dodi go ashore at Monte Carlo

6   Diana and Dodi return to London

7   *Daily Mirror* breaks story linking Diana and Dodi in a relationship

Diana shares dinner with Dodi at his Park Lane apartment – she arrives home after 1 a.m.

8   Diana travels to Bosnia on a 3 day anti-landmine campaign trip. She communicates with Dodi regularly by satellite mobile phone.

10   Diana returns to London from Bosnia

"The Kiss" photo is published by the *Sunday Mirror*

Diana and Dodi travel to Mohamed's Oxted estate. They stay overnight

11   Diana and Dodi return to London from Oxted

12   Diana travels again with Dodi to Oxted, where they stay two nights

13   Diana and Dodi travel from Oxted by helicopter to see psychic counsellor Rita Rogers. They later return to Oxted

Diana gives Dodi her father's cufflinks

14   Diana and Dodi return to London from Oxted. They share dinner at Dodi's apartment before attending a private pre-release screening of the movie *Air Force One*

15   Diana flies to Greece with Rosa Monckton, commencing a 6 day holiday sailing around the Greek Islands

Dodi's possessions unpacked at Malibu

16   Discussions between Dodi and his assistant, Melissa Henning, to upgrade security at Malibu to cater for Diana living there

18   Dodi phones Ritz Hotel President, Frank Klein, in Antibes to tell him he and Diana will need accommodation in Paris around the end of August

US President, Bill Clinton, announces his agreement to sign anti-landmine treaty

20	Diana returns to London, and visits Dodi's apartment
21	Diana meets with her local Anglican priest, then goes to her gym, visits her Chinese doctor, before later spending time at Dodi's apartment
22	Diana and Dodi commence a 9 day holiday aboard the *Jonikal* in the Mediterranean
	Dodi tells John Johnson he will be needed on security in Malibu
23	Diana and Dodi go ashore at Monte Carlo and visit Repossi Jewellers
27	*Le Monde* quotes Diana describing the previous Conservative government as "hopeless" on landmines
30	Diana and Dodi fly from Sardinia to Paris, landing at Le Bourget Airport at 3.20 p.m.
31	Princess Diana and Dodi Fayed die following a 12.23 a.m. car crash in the Alma Tunnel, Paris
	Early edition *Mirror* article states that next week's WAG meeting will table an MI6 report on the Fayeds and will discuss the Harrods royal warrants
	French crash investigation begins

Sep

2	Simmons burns up her copy of Diana's anti-landmine dossier
	Judge Hervé Stéphan is appointed to head the French investigation
17	Treaty banning landmines endorsed by 90 countries, including UK, in Oslo, Norway. USA pulls out after having earlier agreed to join the ban. Clinton says: "There is a line I simply cannot cross"
	Mishcon delivers to MPS Commissioner, Paul Condon, 1995 notes revealing that Diana predicted her death by staged car crash. Condon locks them in his safe for six years

1999

Mar 1	UK ratifies treaty banning the import, export, transfer and manufacture of landmines

TIMELINE

Sep 3   French investigation ends, concluding that the crash was caused by a drunk driver, Henri Paul, who was also speeding

2002

Mar   Royal coroner John Burton resigns. He is replaced by Michael Burgess

2003

Oct 20   Book written by Diana's butler, Paul Burrell, includes the publication of a note written by Diana accusing Prince Charles of planning her death in a car crash

2004

Jan

6   British inquest into the deaths of Diana and Dodi opens

Burgess requests the British police to conduct a full inquiry into the deaths

Inquest is adjourned

7   MPS Commissioner John Stevens is appointed head of Operation Paget, the British inquiry.

2006

Jul 22   Royal coroner Michael Burgess resigns from the case, citing a heavy workload.

Sep 7   Appointment of Elizabeth Butler-Sloss as new coroner

Dec 14   British inquiry ends and the Paget report is published. Stevens concludes that the crash was caused by a drunk driver, Henri Paul, who was also speeding

2007

Apr 24   Elizabeth Butler-Sloss resigns as coroner for the case, citing inexperience with the jury system

Jun   Scott Baker takes over as coroner

Oct 2   British inquest main hearings begin with an 11 person jury

2008

Apr 7   British inquest concludes with the jury's verdict that the crash was caused by "unlawful killing, grossly negligent driving of the following vehicles and of the Mercedes"

8   Worldwide media reports alter the wording of the verdict to read "paparazzi" instead of "following vehicles"

1 Annus Horribilus

1992 was the year that shocked Queen Elizabeth.

The Queen now realised that her once highly-prized daughter-in-law – Princess Diana – had the power to unleash irreparable damage to her royal family.

The seeds to this annus horribilus – year of disaster – had been sown in an earlier period. The Squidgy tapes – "bloody hell, after all I've done for this fucking family" – published in August 1992, were recordings of a conversation between Diana and her long-time friend, James Gilbey, made on New Year's Eve 1990.

But of even more consequence was an Andrew Morton article that appeared in London's *Sunday Times* during March 1991. Based on information deliberately leaked from Diana – via her close friend, Dr James Colthurst – it revealed insider details of the situation in the Charles-Diana household.

Meanwhile, in late 1990, Rosa Monckton – married to *Sunday Telegraph* editor and MI6 agent, Dominic Lawson – was developing a friendship with the newly-arrived Brazilian ambassador's wife, Lucia Flecha de Lima. Rosa, who had been managing director of Tiffany's London since 1986, first met Lucia after employing her daughter, Beatriz.

Several months later, in April 1991, Lucia and her ambassador-husband, Paulo, were scheduled to accompany Diana and Charles on an official visit to their homeland, Brazil. Lucia told royal journalist, Richard Kay, in 2003: "The first thing Diana said to me was: 'You are Lucia. I've been told we should become good friends.'" Lucia also told Kay that "a mutual friend suggested to me that I would be a 'good help' to Diana".

After returning from Brazil the Diana-Lucia friendship developed. "Our friendship grew stronger and stronger", Lucia told the police in 2004.

Later in 1991, Rosa – whose brother Anthony Monckton had been an MI6 officer since 1987 – asked Lucia for an introduction to Princess Diana. Maybe Lucia was reluctant, but eventually Rosa got her way.

Rosa's first meeting with Diana was to be lunch with Lucia in February 1992 – the second month of the Queen's annus horribilus.

While Rosa had been busy trying to arrange an audience with the princess, Diana herself had been just as preoccupied with trying to anonymously tell the world about the hell her life was in the royal family.

Diana had married her prince charming, Charles, a decade earlier. But there was a huge problem. Diana was deeply in love with Charles ... but the feeling was not reciprocal. In fact, it was worse, Charles was in love with an entirely different woman – Camilla Parker-Bowles.

Diana did provide a very useful service for the royals – "an heir and a spare" (princes William and Harry) – but that was about as far as it went.

Charles never really left Camilla and after Harry was born in 1984 Diana said "it just went bang, our marriage, the whole thing went down the drain".

Charles had performed his duty. He and Diana had created the heir and spare and it seemed he now no longer needed Diana, whom he had never been in love with anyway – "whatever love means".

Diana found herself trapped in a loveless marriage, with very little, if any, support from her royal family ... but worse, with the whole world watching her every move. It's little wonder that by 1991, seven years down the track, after media reports and books putting the official royal viewpoint, Diana was desperate for people – the public – to somehow be made aware of her diabolical situation.

Enter: friend, James Colthurst and writer, Andrew Morton.

In mid-1991, a couple of months after the Diana-Lucia Brazil trip, Colthurst started recording secret interviews with Diana, in her Kensington Palace sitting room – on behalf of Morton. Princess Diana was taking the first tentative steps towards revealing to the world the story of her appalling treatment at the hands of the royal family.

Very little in Diana's life was completely secret, because she was under constant surveillance by British intelligence.

In November that year, Andrew Morton's office in central London was burgled – "files rifled through" he later wrote. And during the following month, December 1991, Diana was warned by her private secretary, Patrick Jephson, that the "men in grey suits" knew about her involvement with the Morton book.

Two months later – in February – Rosa Monckton met Diana for the first time.

The serialisation of Andrew Morton's book *Diana: Her True Story* began in the *Sunday Times* on 7 June 1992. Eleven days later Diana received a bombshell letter from Prince Philip.

Diana was shocked. She "was so alarmed ... that she ... asked [a friend] to recommend a solicitor to help draft a suitable reply", Morton later wrote. Her friend, Lucia – who did actually help Diana with the reply – concurred that she "was quite upset".

Diana did reply three days later, on June 21, and that triggered a series of letters over the next six weeks, which included discussion of the issues in the Diana-Charles marriage. The true nature and contents of those letters has never been revealed.

"Squidgy" followed, published in *The Sun* in late August – with an accompanying phone number where people could hear for themselves the Diana-Gilbey recordings.

In November, the Queen set up the Way Ahead Group and on the 24th announced to the world her "annus horribilus".

Just two weeks after that, the official separation of Diana and Charles was announced in the British Parliament.

The collaborative involvement of Diana in the Morton book had forever changed the dynamics of her relationships with the Queen and Philip. Never before had a senior royal divulged so much inside information to the British public – details of the relationship between Charles and Camilla, Diana's own battle with bulimia and her desperate attempts to suicide.

Very soon after that June publication Diana found herself ostracised by the royals at Ascot and her use of the Queen's Flight and the Royal Train was permanently restricted.

The Way Ahead Group (WAG), which was created five months later to deal with major issues facing the royals, held meetings twice a year – generally in January and September. Those meetings were attended by all senior royals, except Diana. The Queen was chairman, with Philip, Charles, Anne, Andrew and Edward all taking part.

It is no coincidence that the separation of Charles and Diana took place in the month following the very first WAG meeting.

By the conclusion of the annus horribilus, Rosa Monckton had manufactured a friendship with Diana; the public knew a great deal more about how things worked within the royal family; the Queen had set up a mechanism for dealing with any future problems – the WAG; and Diana had been removed from the royal inner sanctum.

"These were dangerous times. The knives were being sharpened for the Princess…."

- Ken Wharfe – Diana's bodyguard, referring to 1992

2   Fear and Surveillance

In August 1993 Rosa Monckton organised a holiday to Bali and Moyo Island – herself, Diana, Lucia and Beatriz.

Lucia said later that "after 12 hours, [Diana] wanted to come home".

Diana did actually stay for five days, but it appears that for 4½ of those, she didn't want to be there.

At that stage the Charles-Diana separation was complete, but there were still issues over the children, and no doubt whether this was going to stay as a separation, or end in divorce.

It is possible Rosa had been sent on a mission – to establish how Diana was thinking, maybe to pressure her to stay in the marriage.

Did Diana smell a rat?

Lucia told the police that "Diana thought maybe Rosa did have a hidden agenda".

Whatever the case, Rosa organised the holiday and 12 hours after arriving, Diana no longer wanted to be there.

Four months after that holiday Diana dispensed with her police royalty protection.

Diana believed she was under surveillance – 18 separate witnesses have stated that's what she told them. And indeed the evidence shows Diana was – right up until the day she was killed in Paris.

Intelligence agencies had bugged Diana's home and had been listening into her phone conversations for years.

In late 1995, events in Diana's life took a dangerous turn.

During October Diana made two critical moves that revealed she could be the target in a future orchestrated car crash.

Princess Diana penned a note which she passed to her butler, Paul Burrell, for safe-keeping.

"I am sitting here at my desk today in October, longing for someone to hug me and encourage me to keep strong and hold my head high – this particular phase of my life is the most dangerous – my husband is planning 'an accident' in my car, brake failure and serious head injury in order to make the path clear for Charles to marry Tiggy [Legge-Bourke]. Camilla is nothing but a decoy.....

"I have been battered, bruised and abused mentally by a system for 15 years now, but I feel no resentment, I carry no hatred, I am weary of the battles, but I will never surrender. I am strong inside and maybe that is a problem for my enemies.

"Thank you Charles, for putting me through such hell and for giving me the opportunity to learn from the cruel things you have done to me. I have gone forward fast and have cried more than anyone will ever know. The anguish nearly killed me, but my inner strength has never let me down, and my guides have taken such good care of me up there. Aren't I fortunate to have had their wings to protect me...."

And, just to make sure, Diana repeated similar fears during a meeting with her lawyer, Victor Mishcon, on October 30. Mishcon wrote up notes:

"HRH said that she had been informed by reliable sources ... that (a) The Queen would be abdicating in April and the Prince of Wales would then assume the throne and (b) efforts would be made if not to get rid of her (be it by some accident in her car such as pre-prepared brake failure or whatever) between now and then, then at least to see that she was so injured or damaged as to be declared 'unbalanced'. She was convinced that there was a conspiracy and that she and Camilla were to be 'put aside'. She had also been told that Miss Legge-Bourke had been operated on for an abortion and that she (HRH) would shortly be in receipt of a 'certificate'....

"HRH, in answer to a question I put to her, said that in her view the happiest solution for the future of the monarchy was for the Prince of Wales to abdicate in favour of Prince William and that

without any malice whatsoever she wished to put that view forward in the interests of the Royal Family and everyone.
"She was disappointed that the Prime Minister [John Major] had not been to see her or got in touch with her for a very considerable time."

There are differing claims in these two documents and some of them did not occur. But there is one factor that is consistent with both – and that essentially did come to pass: "'an accident' in my car, brake failure and serious head injury"; "some accident in her car such as pre-prepared brake failure".

The very next month – November 1995 – the brakes in Diana's Audi did fail.

Diana's friend, Simone Simmons, recounts the incident in her 2005 book:

"As she approached a set of traffic lights which had just turned to red, she put her foot on the brake but nothing happened and the car kept coasting forward. When it eventually came to a halt she leapt out, abandoned [her car] where it was, and went straight back to Kensington Palace in a taxi, whose driver refused to accept his fare, and asked for her autograph instead. She rang me and said, 'Someone's tampered with my brakes'....
"[After this] she wrote to her friends Lady Annabel Goldsmith, Lucia Flecha de Lima and Elsa Bowker. She also wrote to me. In the letter I received she warned, 'The brakes on my car have been tampered with. If something does happen to me it will be MI5 or MI6.'"

Diana also informed other people: Hasnat Khan, her boyfriend; Paul Burrell, her butler; and Patrick Jephson, her private secretary.

But November 1995 was to become famous for a different reason.

Diana launched a second attack on the royals – this time, not as a silent partner to a best-selling book, but in a very personal, prime-time television interview: *Panorama*.

Princess Diana spoke directly to the nation:
- "There were three of us in this marriage, so it was a bit crowded"

- "Anything good I ever did nobody ever said a thing. Never said, 'well done', or 'was it OK?' But if I tripped up, which invariably I did, because I was new at the game, a ton of bricks came down on me"

- "I am a very strong person – and I know that causes complications in the system that I live in"

- "People's agendas changed overnight [post-separation]. I was now separated wife of the Prince of Wales – I was a problem, I was a liability (seen as), and 'How are we going to deal with her? This hasn't happened before.'"

- "Visits abroad being blocked [post-separation] ... things that had come naturally my way being stopped, letters going, that got lost.... Everything changed after we separated, and life became very difficult then for me"

- Squidgygate "was done to harm me in a serious manner, and that was the first time I'd experienced what it was like to be outside the net, so to speak, and not be in the family.... It was to make the public change their attitude towards me.... It was, you know, if we are going to divorce, my husband would hold more cards than I would"

- "I'll fight to the end, because I believe that I have a role to fulfil, and I've got two children to bring up"

- "The enemy was my husband's department, because I always got more publicity. My work was more, was discussed much more than him"

- "I'd like to be a queen of people's hearts, in people's hearts, but I don't see myself being Queen of this country"

- "I would think that the top job, as I call it, would bring enormous limitations to [Charles] and I don't know whether he could adapt to that".

That same night, following *Panorama*, close friend of Charles and Britain's Minister for the Armed Forces, Nicholas Soames, went on *Newsnight* and said: Diana "really is [in] the advanced stages of paranoia".

The day following *Panorama* going to air, Diana travelled to Buenos Aires with her friend, Roberto Devorik, an Argentinian fashion designer. She spoke to William by phone, then told Devorik: "I am sure that Prince Philip is involved with the security services. After this, they are going to get rid of me."

Philip did retaliate and was more vicious this time.

Simone Simmons saw the letters: They "were the nastiest letters Diana had ever received. She had death threats which were worded nicer than [Philip's] letters. He called her a trollop and a harlot and said she was damaging the Royal Family."

While Diana's post-*Panorama* public support soared to 85%, the Queen was busy working out how to respond.

In December she acted.

The Queen punished the BBC for airing the program – she withdrew their sole broadcast rights to her annual Christmas message.

Then, within three weeks of *Panorama* the Queen was in negotiations with prime minister, John Major, and the Archbishop of Canterbury, George Carey, trying to establish a way to enforce a Diana-Charles divorce. On 18 December 1995 – just under a month after she had gone public – Diana received a letter from the Queen requesting the divorce.

Eight months later – on 28 August 1996 – the Diana-Charles divorce was made final. But the Queen added extras – she stripped Diana of her HRH title and effectively removed her from the royal family.

Meanwhile Diana's fears increased.

Roberto Devorik described a luncheon conversation in the spring of 1996, where the actress Isabelle Huppert invited Diana to attend the play *Mary, Queen of Scots*. Devorik said Diana replied: "I really would prefer not to see the play. I know the ending and I will finish like Mary, Queen of Scots, and be chopped. I am an inconvenience for them."

Devorik also stated that Diana, around the same time, told him: "Prince Philip wants to see me dead".

He testified that he was sitting with Diana in the VIP area of an airport lounge in June 1996, when "she pointed to the portrait of Prince Philip and said, 'He really hates me and would like to see me disappear'".

Other witnesses have sworn on oath that there were difficulties in the Philip-Diana relationship – her close friends Susan Kassem and Hasnat Khan.

Simmons' account of seeing letters from Philip worded worse than death threats raises the question: If Philip was prepared to put that much vitriol against Diana in writing, how much more threatening would his verbal confrontations with her have been?

Devorik's evidence provides the answer – "Prince Philip wants to see me dead".

Devorik also said that in 1996 Diana's fears extended to others – particularly Nicholas Soames, then Minister of the Armed Forces and Robert Fellowes, her brother-in-law and private secretary to the Queen. Diana said of Fellowes: "He hates me. He will do anything to get me out of the Royals. He cost me the friendship with my sister [Jane]".

Raine Spencer, Diana's step-mother, related to the inquest that Jane, who was Fellowes' wife had told her that "because of her husband's position, she could not see [Diana] anymore".

During this period Diana's boyfriend, Dr Hasnat Khan, was receiving death threats. He told the police: "I ... received envelopes containing cut-out pictures of me, together with a noose around my neck. This went on and on and it was very stressful."

The Diana-Charles divorce – and exclusion from the royal family – provided Diana with the freedom from the royal cage that she had so desperately needed.

Witnesses who were asked described the post-divorce Diana as free and happy – "glowing"; "very happy, very glamorous and great fun"; "she became much more focused.... It was time to go forward".

But the Queen – the very person who had brought on the divorce – now had a new problem.

Post-divorce Diana was flying free and basically operating outside of the Queen's control. By excluding Diana from the royal family, the Queen had effectively exhausted her own legal options for punishing any "misbehaviour". This meant that if Diana .misbehaved the Queen had placed herself in a position where she would potentially have to consider illegal actions against Diana.

During the latter half of 1996 Diana began to involve herself in the international campaign to ban landmines. Her friend, Simone Simmons, who was aware of the landmine research Diana was conducting, received this special message in her 1996 Christmas card: "The knowledge is expanding at alarming speed. Watch out world."

Two critical factors – the enforced expulsion from the royal family and Diana's move to become the public face of the anti-landmine campaign – were destined to have far-reaching consequences in the following year....

"The Queen is disgusted with [Diana] and wishes she'd just go away"
- *Time* magazine, 11 December 1995, quoting a "veteran royal watcher"

"I really feel the girl has been bad news.... Frankly, the sooner [Diana] emigrates to the United States the better. She has done the institution of our constitutional monarchy considerable damage."
- Michael Colvin, chairman of the Defence Select Committee and the Foreign Affairs Committee, June 1996

3   Flying Free

On 12 January 1997 Princess Diana landed in Angola on a mission to help landmine victims and campaign for the worldwide eradication of anti-personnel landmines.

Soon after arriving Diana spoke to the assembled international media:

> "It is an enormous privilege for me to be invited here to Angola, in order to assist the Red Cross in its campaign to ban once and for all anti-personnel landmines. There couldn't be a more appropriate place to begin this campaign than Angola, because this nation has the highest number of amputees per population than anywhere in the world. By visiting Angola, we shall gain an understanding of the plight of the victims of landmines and how survivors are helped to recover from their injuries. We'll also be able to observe the wider implications of these devastating weapons on the life of this country as a whole. It is my sincere hope that by working together in the next few days we shall focus world attention on this vital but, until now, largely neglected issue."

Diana stayed in Angola for four days, but the trip caused a furore amongst Conservative politicians back in the United Kingdom. Earl Howe, the Junior Defence Minister, stated publicly that Diana "is ill-advised and is not being helpful or realistic.... We do not need a loose cannon like her".

Four days after Diana returned to the UK, the Queen convened a meeting of the Way Ahead Group in Buckingham Palace.

Then during the following month – February 1997 – Diana received a threatening phone call at her home in Kensington Palace. Her friend Simone Simmons was there:

"I was with Diana in her sitting-room at KP when she beckoned me over and held her large old-fashioned black telephone away from her ear so that I could hear. I heard a voice telling her she should stop meddling with things she didn't understand or know anything about, and spent several minutes trying to tell her to drop her [anti-landmines] campaign. Diana didn't say much, she just listened, and I clearly heard the warning: 'You never know when an accident is going to happen.' [Diana] went very pale. The moment she put the phone down we started talking about what he had said. I tried to be reassuring which was not easy – she was clearly very worried....

"When I listened into her conversation, with its apparent warning ... I was not sure [of her safety] any more. The conversation frightened Diana, and it certainly scared me."

Diana told Simmons that the caller was the Minister of the Armed Forces and close long-time friend of Prince Charles, Nicholas Soames – the same person who just 14 months earlier had accused Diana on national TV of being in "the advanced stages of paranoia".

Diana was not deterred and said to Simmons: "It doesn't matter what happens to me. We must do something. We cannot allow this slaughter to continue."

Then following the Soames phone call, Diana sought out a way of secretly recording her story. On March 7 a former BBC cameraman met with Diana at Kensington Palace and recorded the first of 7 videos. By the time the recordings were complete – later in March – there was 12 hours of footage. She addressed her 17 years of mistreatment at the hands of the royal family and also problems within the family, including her concerns regarding the relationship between Prince Charles and his senior valet, Michael Fawcett.

Meanwhile Princess Diana spent months building up an anti-landmine dossier, made up of sourced information and her own handwritten notes. As a precaution she kept it in her friend Elsa Bowker's locked safe. Then in June – after the dossier had grown to be several inches thick – Diana took a copy of it, which she gave to

Simmons for safe-keeping. Simmons hid "it at the head of [her] bed underneath the mattress".

On 1 May 1997 Tony Blair was installed as UK Prime Minister following a landslide election result in favour of New Labour. With that, Nicholas Soames' party lost power and Britain resolved to sign the upcoming anti-landmine treaty.

Diana delivered a landmark anti-landmine speech at the Royal Geographic Society in London on June 12. It was entitled: "Responding to Landmines: A Modern Tragedy and Its Consequences". This was to be Diana's final major address against the proliferation of landmines.

She said:

"The world is too little aware of the waste of life, limb and land which anti-personnel landmines are causing among some of the poorest people on earth....

"For the mine is a stealthy killer. Long after conflict is ended, its innocent victims die or are wounded singly, in countries of which we hear little. Their lonely fate is never reported. The world, with its many other preoccupations, remains largely unmoved by a death roll of something like 800 people every month – many of them women and children. Those who are not killed outright – and they number another 1,200 a month – suffer terrible injuries and are handicapped for life.

"I was in Angola in January with the British Red Cross.... Some people chose to interpret my visit as a political statement. But it was not. I am not a political figure. As I said at the time, and I'd like to reiterate now, my interests are humanitarian. That is why I felt drawn to this human tragedy. This is why I wanted to play down my part in working towards a world-wide ban on these weapons....

"The human pain that has to be borne is often beyond imagining.... That is something to which the world should urgently turn its conscience.

"In Angola, one in every 334 members of the population is an amputee. Angola has the highest rate of amputees in the world. How can countries which manufacture and trade in these weapons square their conscience with such human devastation?...

"Much ingenuity has gone into making some of these mines. Many are designed to trap an unwary de-miner.... I reflected, after my visit to Angola, if some of the technical skills used in making mines had been applied to better methods of removing them....

"These mines inflict most of their casualties on people who are trying to meet the elementary needs of life. They strike the wife, or the grandmother, gathering firewood for cooking. They ambush the child sent to collect water for the family....

"One of the main conclusions I reached after this experience: Even if the world decided tomorrow to ban these weapons, this terrible legacy of mines already in the earth would continue to plague the poor nations of the globe. 'The evil that men do, lives after them.'

"And so, it seems to me, there rests a certain obligation upon the rest of us.

"One of my objectives in visiting Angola was to forward the cause of those, like the Red Cross, striving in the name of humanity to secure an international ban on these weapons. Since then, we are glad to see, some real progress has been made. There are signs of a change of heart – at least in some parts of the world. For that we should be cautiously grateful. If an international ban on mines can be secured it means, looking far ahead, that the world may be a safer place for this generation's grandchildren.

"But for this generation in much of the developing world, there will be no relief, no relaxation. The toll of deaths and injuries caused by mines already there, will continue....

"I would like to see more done for those living in this 'no man's land', which lies between the wrongs of yesterday and the urgent needs of today.

"I think we owe it. I also think it would be of benefit to us, as well as to them. The more expeditiously we can end this plague on Earth caused by the landmine, the more readily can we set about the constructive tasks to which so many give their hand in the cause of humanity."

Just nine days earlier, on Tuesday June 3, Diana had attended an English National Ballet (ENB) performance of *Swan Lake* at the Royal Albert Hall. This was to be her last visit to the Hall and she was present in her role as ENB patron. At the gala dinner held in the Churchill Hotel following the ballet, Diana was seated next to long-time family friend, Mohamed Al Fayed and his wife, Heini.

During the dinner conversation they discussed the upcoming summer holidays. Diana said she was still working out where to take William and Harry. Mohamed and Heini invited Diana and the boys to join them at their St Tropez villa in July.

Six days later, on Monday the 9th, Diana phoned Michael Cole, Harrods Director of Public Affairs, to find out more detail about the facilities. Then on the Wednesday Diana penned a letter to Mohamed: "Dear Mohamed, A very special thank you indeed for inviting the boys and I to stay in France next month. Needless to say we are greatly looking forward to it all and we are so grateful to you for giving us this opportunity.... I know we will speak soon, but until then, my love to you all, Diana."

Then on the next day, June 12, Diana delivered the significant anti-landmine speech in London – "how can countries which manufacture and trade in these weapons square their conscience"; "the evil that men do"; "this plague on earth caused by the landmine".

In two short days Princess Diana – who was under the constant surveillance of the British security services – had delivered two powerful messages.

First: to the British Establishment, including the royal family. Second: to the leading arms dealing nations of the western world – the US, UK and France.

On Thursday 12 June 1997 Princess Diana effectively declared war on the armaments industries of the US, UK and France – for even though Britain and France were to sign the Ottawa treaty to ban landmines, it was apparent that Diana would not have stopped at landmines: "my interests are humanitarian – that is why I felt drawn to this human tragedy". As a humanitarian, Diana – after succeeding against landmines – would have sought an end to cluster bombs and other evil – "the evil that men do" – weapons.

PARIS-LONDON CONNECTION

On Wednesday 11 June 1997 – after Princess Diana accepted the invitation to take William and Harry to Mohamed's villa – Diana, whether intentionally or not, had made a decision that sent shockwaves into the inner sanctum of the senior royals and the British Establishment.

As far as they were concerned Mohamed Al Fayed was a person of ill repute. They had repeatedly refused British citizenship, despite him having four British children. Mohamed had recently contributed to the downfall of the Tory government with his involvement in the "cash for questions" scandal. And to top it all off, Mohamed was currently under police investigation over an alleged theft – later proven to be false – from a Harrods safety deposit box. This is without adding underlying factors such as Prince Philip's racist attitude – "I can never tell the difference between you chaps". An Egyptian had bought the Harrods store, one of London's jewels. Philip later described Mohamed's son, Dodi, as an "oily bed-hopper".

So for Diana to take the future king – William – on a 10-day holiday with Mohamed Al Fayed was considered a major issue to the Queen. She had the power to veto the trip – the Queen could have prevented her grandsons from travelling to France.

It may be particularly significant that she – wearied now from over five years of trouble from Diana – did not intervene this time.

Two weeks later, Diana was forced to withdraw plans to attend a private All-Party Landmines Eradication Group meeting, held in the House of Commons. Just before the June 25 event Conservative MPs had started protesting. David Wiltshire complained: "She is entering the political process. That raises fundamental questions about the role of the monarchy." No one mentioned the fact that the Queen had met the prime minister every week for the previous 40 years.

Just a few days after that, while in Hong Kong for the 30 June 1997 handover – also attended by senior MI6 officer, Sherard Cowper-Coles – Rosa Monckton phoned Diana to invite her on a five day Greek Island cruise, scheduled for mid-August.

This was however no ordinary cruise. Financed by MI6 (as will be revealed) Monckton, who was an agent, had been asked to find out what she could about Diana's intentions and plans.

A week later, on Sunday July 6, Princess Diana was to have her final meeting with the newly-installed prime minister at Chequers. Tony Blair later lied about the content of their private conversation: "I just broached the subject of her and Dodi straight out. She didn't like it and I could feel the wilful side of her bridling. However she didn't refuse to talk about it, so we did, and also what she might do."

Blair made this up.

The problem for Blair is that this conversation took place on July 6 – exactly eight days <u>before</u> Diana first met Dodi, during the St Tropez holiday.

Then two days later a preparatory meeting of the Way Ahead Group (WAG) took place at Buckingham Palace. This was attended by the royal private secretaries and other senior officials and was designed to lay the groundwork for a major WAG meeting set to occur two weeks later. Neither of these meetings had been scheduled in advance – in fact the WAG would normally not have met until September, but the meeting had been brought forward by two months because of the escalating crisis around Diana's activities.

Three days later Diana, William and Harry travelled with Mohamed and his family to the St Tropez villa, beginning the ten day holiday.

David Davies, head of MPS royalty protection, had voiced the concerns of the police to the Queen's private secretary before the trip occurred. Later Davies stated: "I was concerned as to the consequence ... for ... the reputation of the Royal Family.... The future King of England and his brother and the mother were going on holiday with a gentleman who ... I had some concerns about".

Controversy erupted.

Harold Brookes-Baker – editor of *Burke's Peerage* – among others, spoke out: "This is totally irresponsible of the Princess – particularly considering the problems people have faced with the Al Fayed connection. These problems are likely to go on for a lot longer – and so it is important that she and the family she married into should be completely removed from controversy. The controversy this is creating is unnecessary for a family that has already been through so much."

Three days into the holiday, on July 14, the party was joined by Mohamed's son, Dodi. Diana and Dodi first met that afternoon on Mohamed's yacht, the *Jonikal*. Debbie Gribble, the chief stewardess on the boat, later described the scene around that evening's dinner: "They got on well enough, but I didn't think anything of it." Then a full-scale fun food fight developed at the table. "They were chasing each other and laughing and giggling like a couple of kids. Then they wrestled a bit and stopped, just staring at each other.... From that moment on something changed in the way they treated each other.... Something had passed between them – suddenly they seemed to fit as a couple." The following day, July 15: "Everyone else had gone their own way. Diana and Dodi were still deep in conversation. She was talking about her work and travels in India and Africa, and he was enthralled."

It was during this holiday that big future plans were discussed between Mohamed and Diana – to set up a worldwide hospice network called "Diana Hospices" and a separate charity for the victims of landmines.

After arriving back in London, Diana wrote to Mohamed and Heini: "Thank you both so much for an enjoyable week in France. I cannot tell you how much I loved it... We were given a <u>wonderful</u> and magical week and adored every minute of our stay.... William and Harry and I had the best holiday imaginable and your family made us so welcome." Diana later said it had been the best family holiday of her life.

On the very day of Diana's return, July 20, the *Sunday Mirror* published an article based on leaks from within the royal household: "Speculation about Diana's future, which is as strong at Buckingham Palace as it is in the Princess's camp, comes as plans are made for the next meeting of the Way Ahead Group.... Top of the agenda at the forthcoming meeting is Diana."

Dodi sent bouquets of pink flowers to Kensington Palace and the Diana-Dodi relationship developed quickly, and there were visits to Dodi's Park Lane apartment.

"One does not need to be judgmental about who is to blame for the divorce, but one is entitled to form a view about who is proving more damaging to the Monarchy in the process.... It is time to separate [Diana] irrevocably from the core of the institution which had earlier been so ready to embrace her."
- Lead article in the magazine of the Tory "Way Forward Group"[2] (President: Margaret Thatcher), June 1996

Diana's anti-landmine efforts "don't actually add much to the sum of human knowledge.... This is an important, sophisticated argument. It doesn't help simply to point at the [landmine] amputees and say how terrible it is."
- Peter Viggers, a member of the UK Parliament's Defence Committee, January 1997

---

[2] This group is not to be confused with the royal Way Ahead Group, mentioned earlier.

4　Decision

Just three days after the St Tropez holiday concluded, the full Way Ahead Group meeting – referred to in the *Mirror* article – chaired by the Queen, was held at Balmoral. Diana was discussed and it is around this time – either at the meeting or soon after – the decision was made that the single most dangerous threat to the Monarchy had to go. And the nod was given to MI6.

There had been a long line of headaches that Diana had caused the British Establishment and taking William and Harry on the holiday to Mohamed's villa was really the crossing of the line – a bridge too far. Add to that the growing discontent with Diana's anti-landmine activities amongst the Western arms-dealing nations – primarily the governments of USA, France and UK – and it added up to only one acceptable outcome: she had to be removed from the scene.

Discussions would have occurred – either by phone or in person – between Bill Clinton, Jacques Chirac and Tony Blair. But none of these people had the authority or power to eliminate Princess Diana from the world stage. That power rested in the head of the royal family, the Queen. Only she could authorise the assassination of the most famous and photographed person in the world, the mother of the future King of England, the increasingly powerful Princess Diana.

Blair was the conduit. Chirac and Clinton could vent their frustration over what was perceived as Diana meddling in international affairs. But it was Blair alone who had regular direct access to the Queen. For over 40 years the British prime minister had met weekly – at 6.30 p.m. on Wednesdays – with the Queen. And if out of town, then the PM was required to telephone. Blair would have passed on the other leaders' – and his own – concerns.

But the Queen had her own unease, which had been building up since the 1992 annus horribilus. Five years of mounting difficulties. But 1997 was the year when the most damaging thorn in her side would be extracted. Only then could the royals move forward.

Between the Western leaders and the senior royals, Diana's fate was sealed. And the decision was finalised at some point close to – or at – the special Way Ahead Group meeting held on Wednesday 23 July 1997.

A decision was made to assassinate Princess Diana outside of the UK. There are special provisions built into UK law that allow for illegal acts to become legal if they are carried out overseas by officers of the Crown. It also makes the holding of a fair inquest so much harder if most of the witnesses live in a foreign country – they cannot be summonsed under UK law.

That meant the job had to be carried out by MI6, Britain's foreign intelligence service. This now became MI6's major operation, but nevertheless, information was only provided on a "need to know" basis, in keeping with normal procedure – except even more so, because this was an extremely sensitive project.

The CIA – which has always had a close relationship with MI6 – would have been brought in at the very early planning stage. They had a history of joint operations and both organisations had been involved in a failed attempt to assassinate Iraqi leader, Saddam Hussein, just 15 months earlier. In that case, Saddam discovered the plot and ruthlessly executed all the locals involved.

But this current plot – the assassination of Princess Diana – could not be allowed to fail. Yet it had to be extremely deniable – it was not acceptable to kill Diana and have it credibly linked to British intelligence. So it had to be made to look like an accident.

To achieve this – guaranteed success and extreme deniability – it meant that the complete process had to be thoroughly planned with military precision.

The most deniable form of death is by car accident. Every day about 3,300 people die in road traffic accidents worldwide. So if Diana could be seen by the world to die in a car accident then that was the most deniable procedure that MI6 could achieve.

DECISION

It is no coincidence that the method chosen was the same as Diana had been told by a source or sources, when she penned her note and spoke to her lawyer just under two years earlier. It is possible a decision about how Diana would die had been made back then, but what wasn't known was when and where – that would be determined by events.

Time now began to speed up as events moved rapidly towards the final meeting between two powerful forces ... Diana, Princess of Wales and MI6.

PARIS-LONDON CONNECTION

5   Countdown

The relationship between Diana and Dodi developed quickly and following their return from St Tropez the couple snuck away to Paris for a secret weekend together. Then two days later, on July 29, Diana met with her boyfriend, Hasnat Khan, in Battersea Park. The following day Hasnat saw her for the final time at Kensington Palace. He later told British police: "Diana told me that it was all over between us".

The next day Diana travelled to the south of France with Dodi and they boarded the *Jonikal* at the start of a seven day Mediterranean cruise. It was during that trip that the famous "the kiss" photo was taken. On August 7, the day after Diana and Dodi returned to London, the story of their relationship broke in the *Daily Mirror*. Three days later "the kiss" was published in the *Sunday Mirror* – confirming the veracity of earlier stories that Princess Diana and Dodi Fayed had become an item.

On August 8, the morning after another visit to Dodi's Park Lane apartment, Diana ratcheted up the anti-landmine campaign with a three day visit to the minefields and victims in Bosnia.

After returning on the 10th, Diana spent several days with Dodi, including a stay at Oxted, Mohamed's country estate. It was there that Diana gave Dodi a very special gift, her late father's cufflinks, with an accompanying letter: "Darling Dodi, These cufflinks were the very last gift that I received from the man I loved most in the world – my father – They are given to you as I know how much joy it would give him to know they were in such safe and special hands.... Fondest love, from Diana. x"

PARIS-LONDON CONNECTION

By the end of this period – before August 15 – Diana and Dodi had plans to live together, and were making preparations to move into Julie Andrews' former Malibu home. They also intended to purchase a property in Paris, where they would live part-time.

On Friday August 15 Diana and Rosa Monckton left London on an Al Fayed jet, headed to Athens. This was the start of the Greek Island cruise, which had been organised by Rosa at the end of June.

After arriving in Greece, Diana and Rosa boarded the *Della Grazia*, a 22 metre yacht with three crew, which had been chartered by MI6. This vessel was tracked by three much larger super yachts – also chartered by MI6 – the *Marala*, 59 metres; the *Sunrise*, 90 metres; and the *Sea Sedan,* 55 metres. These super yachts provided security, but also cruised about acting as media decoys.

While Diana and Rosa drifted around the Aegean Sea for five days in the smallish *Della Grazia*, the world's media searched doggedly for the princess. MI6 were so keen to protect Diana's location that they arranged for a decoy article to be published in London, stating that "the two were staying on the remote island of Inousses" – across the other side of the Aegean. But when reporters, including Greek journalists, flocked to that island, Diana was nowhere to be seen and there was also no evidence she had been there.

This gave Rosa five days of peace and quiet alone with Diana – time to cover plenty of territory on plans and intentions and to seek any other intelligence that was relevant for her spy-masters.

Meanwhile Dodi was making arrangements for the next cruise with Diana and on August 18 made a critical call to Frank Klein, president of the Ritz Hotel, Paris. Klein recalled later: Dodi told "me that he intended to come to Paris at the end of the month" accompanied by his "friend", Diana.

US intelligence – NSA, which was monitoring the couple's phone conversations – was then made aware that Princess Diana and Dodi Fayed would be visiting Paris around the end of August. Not only that, but it would have been evident that there would be trips between the Ritz Hotel – an Al Fayed asset – and Dodi's Paris apartment. During the late July weekend when Diana and Dodi had stayed in Paris, both the apartment and hotel had been visited and there had been trips back and forth.

After Frank Klein received the August 18 Dodi communication, his first call was to the Ritz Paris, to his second in command, Claude

Roulet. Klein expected to continue his holiday in Antibes beyond the end of the month – it therefore became Roulet's responsibility to ensure the hotel and staff were readied for the anticipated arrival of the VIPs. Roulet passed on the information to his Ritz security head, Henri Paul, but also notified his intelligence handler. This confirmed the news the agencies had already received, courtesy of the NSA surveillance operation.

From this point on, MI6 – working in conjunction with the CIA and the French intelligence agency, DGSE – set about planning to carry out one of the most significant events of the 20th century, the assassination of Princess Diana.

It was under a month since MI6 had received the nod from senior royals – and now an opportunity to accomplish an extremely deniable operation had opened up. Very close to the chauffeur's route between the Ritz Hotel and Dodi Fayed's apartment lay the Alma Tunnel – a potentially dangerous traffic spot when negotiated at speed. All it required was to prevent the target vehicle, travelling down the riverside expressway, from exiting after the Alexandre III tunnel and it would then be forced into the Alma. With a plan to remove any back-up car, add chasing powerful motorbikes, a strobe light and a waiting vehicle, MI6 began to formulate how this operation could be brought about.

Within hours the top MI6 officer in France, Eugene Curley, received instructions that he was to be heavily involved in orchestrating the assassination of the extremely popular princess. He baulked at this and, despite his 16 years of loyalty in the organisation, refused to participate.

Curley had to be replaced and quickly. Sherard Cowper-Coles, with 20 years' experience, had recently completed the handover of Hong Kong back to the Chinese. He was still based at MI6 headquarters in London. MI6 Chief David Spedding immediately transferred Cowper-Coles into Paris as the replacement head of France. He pulled Curley back into London and a deal was made – Curley could stay in MI6 so long as he would testify on oath to any later investigation that he was still France's MI6 head at the time of the assassination.

Soon after arriving in Paris, Cowper-Coles, comprehending the complexity of the operation, called for more staff. Valerie Caton, who had just come back from leave, was despatched and Spedding also sent over his own personal secretary, Richard Spearman. The rapid transfer of Spearman, who arrived on August 26, five days before the assassination, was a clear signal of how important it was to Spedding that this operation was successful.

Cowper-Coles had a team of at least eight officers based in the Paris embassy. Most, if not all, would have been working on this case, but only two or three – probably Cowper-Coles, Caton and Spearman – would have known ahead of time the precise goal of the operation.

Just as important as having the right staff in the embassy, was the coordination of the roles of agents on the ground in Paris. This required the close cooperation of other agencies, particularly France's DST and DGSE.

Critical to the early planning was the engagement of two Ritz Hotel staff members who were already intelligence agents – Claude Roulet, the vice-president, and Henri Paul, the acting hotel security chief. Neither of these men had any idea what the intelligence chiefs had in mind.

To bring about a successful operation, MI6 also required in Paris about five experienced, proficient riders on powerful motorbikes, a driver and car that would wait near the tunnel ahead of the incident, an emergency response doctor, two ambulance-based doctors (including one dispatcher) for a back-up plan in case Diana survived, a pathologist, a toxicologist and an embalmer.

Ex-MI6 officer, Richard Tomlinson, later told the inquest into the deaths: "MI6 would employ various people [who] would have a full time occupation that they did themselves to earn their living. Their own profession gave them cover and access to do small odd jobs for MI6 around the globe."

Agencies pay well for this work – Henri Paul had built up funds of over 1.2 million French francs (£125,000) in various bank accounts. This, as well as owning a property and the cost involved in regular flying and becoming a pilot. Tomlinson has related an instance of an agent, who helped MI6 obtain key foreign weapons information, being paid £100,000 per year, with special bonuses for difficult jobs of around £500,000.

These people are agents who work for the intelligence agencies. They are handled by the officers, who generally are full-time employees based in embassies or at headquarters.

All of the people needed for this operation were already agents for US, French or British intelligence. Cowper-Coles' job was to establish the detail of the plan and coordinate the resources of the various agencies to complete the operation. It was daunting though, because the time-frame was short. Cowper-Coles was probably on the ground in Paris around the 20th but the targets were expected in about 10 days, just before the end of August. Cowper-Coles would receive updates as the time drew closer – based on surveillance, if there was any expectation of an earlier or delayed arrival, or if the trip was aborted. As it turned out, the timing fitted pretty much with the initial expectation – an arrival in Paris at the end of the month.

On the same day as the Dodi-Klein phone call, August 18 (Washington time), US president, Bill Clinton, announced to the world that he would support an international ban on landmines by the end of the year. Jerry White, co-founder of Land Mine Survivors Network, said: "Princess Di can be very proud. She was central to pushing Clinton off the fence."

Two days later, August 20, Diana and Rosa returned from the cruise to London, and Diana visited Dodi at his Park Lane apartment.

Then, the next day Diana dropped in on her local Anglican priest, Frank Gelli. He later described the meeting: "She stopped by my house on the way to the gym. She wanted to know if it was possible for two people of different religions to marry. I told her it was. As we spoke, [her] telephone rang. It was obviously Dodi. Her eyes lit up. As she was leaving she asked me if I would be able to perform the service when she got married. Her love was obvious. Whenever she mentioned Dodi's name her face lit up. I have only seen that look on the faces of people who are deeply in love."

A day later, Friday August 22, Diana and Dodi embarked on their final cruise together, again on the *Jonikal*, and again in the sparkling summer waters of the Mediterranean.

On Saturday, with the boat moored off Monte Carlo, Diana and Dodi headed for shore. Myriah Daniels, the couple's on board holistic healer, described what happened: "They took off without the bodyguards and the bodyguards were somewhere else in the boat. By the time they said 'Gee, we are going', the guys did not have enough time to get from one end of the boat to the tender to go with them. The bodyguards were livid."

Trixi Chall, a former journalist with the German *Bild* living in Monaco, saw Diana and Dodi come ashore: "I was surprised to see Diana the Princess of Wales hand in hand with a man I had never seen before. It was amazing because there were no bodyguards". Chall says she followed them, observing from the other side of the road. "They went to the shop situated on the left of the Hermitage hotel, which is Repossi the Jeweller. They looked in the window and Diana was pointing with her finger at something." Chall kept walking then turned round and saw the couple entering the Repossi shop.

Claude Roulet later told police that he received a call at the Ritz from Dodi: "The Princess liked a ring that she had seen in the window of the jewellers, Repossi. He asked me to ensure that this ring be available for them in Paris."

Later that day Diana phoned her Anglican priest, Frank Gelli. He later recalled the conversation: "She said she had some very good news and seemed very excited. She invited me to go to Kensington Palace on her return. After all the things that she had previously told me about their relationship, I could only imagine that she was about to announce her engagement to Dodi."

Diana had seen a ring from Repossi's romantic "Dis-Moi-Oui" – "Tell Me Yes" – range of engagement rings.

This same ring was to be purchased by Dodi seven days later in Paris.

Within hours of that purchase, the couple would be dead.

6   Last Days

While Diana and Dodi cruised the Mediterranean on a luxury yacht followed by hordes of international media, Sherard Cowper-Coles worked feverishly in Paris to fulfill his boss, David Spedding's, orders.

With only 10 days to plan and bring the operation to fruition, each waking hour was critical. There were certain factors that were of crucial importance to MI6: a method to divert the vehicle into the Alma Tunnel, there had to be no back-up car, they had to have their own man driving the death car, pointers that publicly turned the crash into an accident had to be in place, a back-up plan just in case the targets survived the crash impact.

As the days progressed, the details emerged.

Motorbike riders could be made to look like paparazzi. One or two motorbikes could block the key expressway exit and force the target car into the tunnel. Control of the post-crash pathology and toxicology could falsely reveal the driver was seriously drunk.

The key plan emerged: the death car followed by frenetic paparazzi who forced a high-speed chase which led the drunk driver to lose control and crash in the tunnel. Yes, the world would accept that. Just a tragic accident brought about by a dreadful mix of circumstances, beyond any living person's control.

MI6 officers soon learned, from Claude Roulet, that there was a particular Mercedes S280 – used by the Ritz – that was parked in the same area of the Vendôme car park every night. It was driven by daytime chauffeur, Olivier Lafaye. Other drivers took their cars home, but Lafaye didn't have a garage, so he left the Mercedes in the car park.

That gave Cowper-Coles his crash car.

Roulet provided MI6 with other vital inside information. Dodi's regular chauffeur was Philippe Dourneau and with Diana in town there would definitely be a back-up car.

A plan outline was developed: Dourneau and the back-up driver would hang out at the front of the Ritz near, or in, their cars. Meanwhile Henri Paul would escort the couple out the back where they would meet the Lafaye Mercedes with no back-up. Henri would drive the crash car.

As the final week progressed this plan would be fleshed out. The actual timing had to wait until Diana and Dodi arrived. But as much as possible was mapped out in advance.

The post-crash detail was worked through.

Dr Frédéric Mailliez, an experienced emergency doctor, would arrive "out of the blue" immediately after the crash. He would take control inside the death car. Dr Jean-Marc Martino, with the help of Dr Arnaud Derossi at SAMU[3] dispatch control, would ensure his was the assigned ambulance for Diana – in case she survived. Dominique Lecomte, head of the IML, who already had form for fixing post-death procedures, would personally conduct all relevant autopsies. Gilbert Pépin would take control of the pathology samples and would be responsible for the key toxicology testing and results. Then, Jean Monceau, experienced embalmer, would carry out whatever was required.

The Mediterranean cruise continued unabated.

Amongst the mass of following paparazzi was French photographer, James Andanson. Andanson was a great lover of things British – born "Jean-Paul", he changed his name to James as an adult. By 1997 Andanson had placed a Union Jack on his central France property and had carried out work for MI6.

Inexplicably, Andanson – who wrote: "the reporting of Lady Di in my eyes is the greatest news story of the last 50 years" – headed for home on August 27, three days before the cruise finished. Andanson never explained why he left early or why he failed to follow Princess Diana to Paris.

Just over 72 hours after Andanson arrived back at his Lignières home, Le Manoir, a car belonging to him – an old-model white Fiat Uno – would be sideswiped by a speeding Mercedes S280 in Paris'

---

[3] The French emergency medical service.

Alma Tunnel. Eye-witnesses would later describe a driver fitting Andanson's description.

During the final week in August the couple's Paris arrival time firmed – it was to be mid-afternoon on Saturday the 30th.

On the Thursday Henri Paul began organising his staff – Didier Gamblin was told he would be required on security at Dodi's 1 Rue Arsène Houssaye apartment from 2 p.m. on Saturday. Philippe Dourneau, Dodi's regular driver, was told the next day, on the Friday, as was Jean-François Musa, the owner-operator of the Étoile fleet that supplied the limousines used by the Ritz. Musa was also a part-time driver for the Ritz and Henri asked him to be on duty from about 5 p.m. Saturday outside the hotel.

Meanwhile on Thursday August 28, Diana celebrated one year since her royal divorce – they went ashore for a beach barbecue. Then the following day, on the Friday evening the *Jonikal* cruise wound down and they anchored near the Sardinian resort of Cala di Volpe.

As Diana and Dodi awoke the next morning, they had no idea that people in Paris were plotting their end and in less than 24 hours they would both be dead.

PARIS-LONDON CONNECTION

7   Saturday August 30

James Andanson was one of the first people to rise that Saturday morning. He had a big day ahead. Andanson left his house, Le Manoir, at about 4.30 a.m. and headed to Vierzon. He never explained this trip, but it is possible he drove his old Fiat Uno, met an accomplice, and had the car loaded onto a train or covered truck bound for Paris. Vierzon is on the Paris train line.

After a peaceful breakfast on the *Jonikal,* Diana, Dodi and entourage left the vessel, loaded themselves and luggage into three taxis and headed for Sardinia's Olbia airport. Their flight destination that day was Paris' Le Bourget.

Henri Paul had a relaxing summer's morning – a game of tennis with his best friend, Claude Garrec, followed by a drink at the Cafe Pelican. Garrec told the police that he "drank a beer and Henri had cola". Then Garrec dropped Henri off outside his apartment at 12.30 p.m. Soon after that Henri's new female friend, Badia Mouhib, phoned him. She later related that he could not see her until after Sunday at 3 p.m. That was just after the time that Diana and Dodi were expected to leave Paris for London.

After lunch, Henri went into work and met with Philippe Dourneau and they headed out to Le Bourget airport to meet the VIPs – Dourneau chauffeuring in the premier vehicle, the Mercedes 600, and Henri driving the back-up Range Rover.

In doing this though, Henri's behaviour was most unusual – even unprecedented.

Ritz president, Frank Klein, later said that Henri was not even meant to be at work that weekend – "no, he was not on duty". Yet his close friend, Dr Dominique Mélo, said: "As soon as Henri learned Dodi and Diana were coming to Paris, he cancelled a short break that he had fixed in Lorient to see his parents."

But much more than that, witnesses stated that in Henri's 11 years working for the Ritz, he had never before driven guests on behalf of the hotel. This was to be the first time.

On top of all that, Henri's friends said that he didn't like driving and tried to avoid it wherever possible. Garrec told the police: "If he could let someone else drive, he would, or if he could avoid driving he would."

So Henri was not meant to be working, never drove Ritz vehicles, and hated driving.

Yet on Friday he had told Jean-François Musa, the back-up driver, not to come in until 5 p.m. Saturday – thus leaving himself the opening to be the back-up driver for the 3 p.m. arrival of the VIPs from Sardinia.

It was an important part of the MI6 plan that Henri got to chat with Dodi immediately after they landed at Le Bourget airport – and photos show Henri, even though he wasn't Dodi's chauffeur, doing just that.

Figure 1 | Dodi Fayed listening intently to what Henri Paul has to say immediately after Diana and Dodi's arrival at Le Bourget airport on 30 August 1997.

Rene Delorm, Dodi's butler, stated: "My boss stopped to talk to a heavy-set balding man in a grey suit and dark glasses. It was Henri Paul."

Why was it so important for Henri to talk to Dodi?

It is impossible to know exactly what was said as both witnesses – Henri and Dodi – died later that night. But it is clear that it was not in the Ritz's interests for Henri to be driving the back-up car – he was not a chauffeur. It is then common sense that Henri was doing this on behalf of his other employer, MI6. The conversation must have been aimed at procuring smooth running of the MI6 plan for the assassination. Henri would have been told what to say and it could have been along the lines of: "We're expecting a lot of pressure from the paparazzi on the ground and we have the security in hand. Please just trust us if we have to make recommendations on actions to take during your stay here to ensure the complete safety of you and the princess."

It was critical to the MI6 plan that Dodi would make decisions based on information from their agents, Claude Roulet and Henri Paul. Later that day, Henri and Roulet provided advice to Dodi – which he did follow – and it led directly to the deaths of Diana, Dodi and Henri.

The Al Fayed Gulfstream jet touched down at Le Bourget at 3.20 p.m.

Waiting was a clutch of paparazzi, a police car and several police motorbikes that provided an escort for the initial part of the journey. French police would later falsely claim that, before the crash occurred, they were completely unaware of Princess Diana's presence in Paris.

Somewhere outside the airport perimeter the police escort peeled away and the procession – the Mercedes 600 with the couple, the Range Rover carrying staff and luggage, several paparazzi vehicles – was joined by a few unidentified, threatening vehicles.

Bodyguard, Trevor Rees-Jones, who was in the lead vehicle, later wrote that "they were surrounded by screaming motorcycles darting around the target vehicles, sometimes two to a bike".

Philippe Dourneau, the Mercedes driver, said people on the motorbikes "were taking pictures. They were hampering us. I remember the flashes of the cameras".

No pictures from this trip have ever been published because the motorbikes surrounding the vehicles were not ridden by paparazzi, but instead intelligence agents posing as paparazzi. The true paparazzi – who were later identified – were following behind the two lead vehicles, expecting to get their photos at the destination. That was the normal procedure.

Kez Wingfield, the bodyguard in the Range Rover later said: "This was the first time in my experience that I had seen the paparazzi behaving so dangerously". That's because they weren't true paparazzi. He said that the paparazzi-hardened Diana later told him "she was concerned that one of the chaps on the motorbikes was going to fall under one of our vehicles".

It should have been a simple airport to city transfer with following paparazzi, but it turned into a frenzied and even dangerous undertaking.

This was just the start of the MI6 plan to create a situation where the paparazzi, throughout that afternoon and night, were seen to be more aggressive and dangerous than they actually are. Later the true paparazzi would have the responsibility for the fatal crash falsely pinned on them.

During this trip, Henri Paul, who had been instructed by MI6 to drive the Range Rover, took drastic evasive action in a successful attempt to divert some of the following vehicles. Fabrice Chassery, one of the genuine paparazzi, told the police: "Suddenly the Range Rover, which was 200 metres in front, effected a sudden, even dangerous manoeuvre, going from the extreme left-hand lane to leave directly towards Neuilly."

The Range Rover, carrying staff and luggage, then proceeded to Dodi's apartment. Dourneau, in the Mercedes, finally shook off the other pursuers and took the couple to a separate Al Fayed property, Villa Windsor in Bois de Boulogne.

Henri Paul and Kez Wingfield offloaded and then proceeded to reconnect with the Mercedes at the Villa.

Diana and Dodi spent about half an hour surveying the Villa Windsor and its contents – with a view to possibly using furniture from it. At an earlier stage, Dodi had thought the Villa could serve as their future Paris residence. But, Diana, who had been through it during their July visit, found it was not the sort of place she wanted to live in – it was "full of ghosts".

From the Villa Windsor, the destination was the Ritz Hotel and the couple entered the rear of the building at 4.35 p.m.

Some of the paparazzi, who had followed the Range Rover from the airport, were already at the Ritz. Other paparazzi had started assembling out the front from about 4 p.m.

But it was going to be a long night.

Inside the hotel Princess Diana had her hair done and made a few phone calls. At 5.30 p.m. she called her UK clairvoyant, Rita Rogers, and amongst other things told her they would be "having dinner at the Ritz".

Claude Roulet suggested to Dodi they should come up with a decoy plan for the dinner arrangements to divert the paparazzi. The idea was to let it be known they were going to a local restaurant called Chez Benoît – when in fact their intention was to return for dinner at the hotel, after spending time at Dodi's apartment. This decoy plan would also be used much later, as part of the cover-up, to falsely suggest that it would have been impossible for MI6 to have known the couple would return to the Ritz.

Throughout the afternoon it became increasingly apparent to MI6 that their original expectation of trips between the hotel and the apartment was correct. With feedback from their agents, Roulet and Henri, and the Diana-Rogers call, it was clear that there would be a Ritz dinner that night. That then also indicated a late-night journey from the hotel to the apartment, where the couple's luggage was. A late night trip was ideal, as it minimised the witnesses – which had also been one of the attractions of a tunnel location.

By around 5 p.m. it became "all systems go" to carry out the assassination operation. Nothing could be left to chance. Some motorbike riders with their pillion photographers had already caused havoc for the VIPs on the streets of the capital. James Andanson travelled the 200 km to Paris. The SAMU doctors and Mailliez were notified to be ready for action later that night. The IML pathologist, Dominique Lecomte, had to be prepared for an early morning call out.

All these people would be handsomely rewarded for fulfilling their crucial parts.

During that late afternoon, Dodi's primary concern was to purchase the Repossi engagement ring, "Tell Me Yes" – the one Diana had seen a week earlier in the Monte Carlo window. Alberto Repossi travelled to Paris, from Monaco, to open their Place Vendôme store especially for Dodi. Dodi visited the shop at 5.45 p.m., but Alberto, who had also employed extra staff for the viewing, was in no mood to allow Dodi to purchase what he saw as a cheap ring, FF115,000 (£12,000). Alberto later said: "I thought that for a lady like the Princess of Wales, we could have given a ring which was the same size but more significant". So five minutes later, after only being shown other more expensive rings, Dodi left the store empty-handed.

It took another hour of Claude Roulet toing and froing between the Ritz and Repossi's before Alberto relented and handed over the ring Dodi had requested. Roulet finally delivered the Tell Me Yes engagement ring to Dodi in the Imperial Suite at 6.45 p.m.

Twelve minutes later, at precisely 6.57 p.m., Diana and Dodi left the hotel, using the rear exit – they were headed for Dodi's apartment. This time Jean-François Musa drove the back-up Range Rover. And they were followed by the ever-present paparazzi, but MI6's fake paparazzi also joined the fray. One of the normal paparazzi, Fabrice Chassery, referred to them as "fans" – he told the French police: "the fans were behaving like madmen". Again photos that have never been published were taken and after they arrived at the apartment Rees-Jones said he told the paparazzi "not to take photographs while we were travelling". This intrusive and disturbing behaviour was a continuation of the MI6 plan to build a false perception of paparazzi that were wildly out of control.

Diana and Dodi arrived at the apartment at about 7.15 p.m. Rene Delorm, Dodi's butler, later said that while there, Dodi showed him the engagement ring. After the crash, the Tell Me Yes ring was found by Delorm in the apartment.

The couple spent over two hours relaxing and before departing Dodi spoke in private to Delorm: "Rene, have some champagne ready because when we come back, I am going to propose to the Princess."

Dodi's uncle, Haseen Yassim, who was staying in Paris, was called by Dodi at 8.45 p.m. with an invitation to meet them for after-dinner coffee in the Ritz Hotel restaurant.

By 9.30 p.m., when Diana and Dodi left the apartment, some of the people involved – even the Mercedes driver, Dourneau – still believed the destination was the decoy restaurant, Chez Benoît. Others, like the two bodyguards and Musa, the Range Rover driver, say they were not told where they were going.

One of the advantages of choosing Chez Benoît as the decoy restaurant was that from the apartment it was in the same general direction as the Ritz – so even after setting out, observers would have believed that the Mercedes was heading to Chez Benoît, even though it actually was going to the Ritz.

The convoy was again accompanied by MI6's fake paparazzi. Philippe Dourneau told the French police: "There were lots of paparazzi. They were coming from all angles, from front and behind. They were all over the place". Jean-François Musa, the back-up car driver, said: "There were paparazzi taking photographs". But again, no photos of this trip – which would have been worth a fortune – have ever been published.

This was the last drive before the final journey and it was important for MI6 to cement the false perception that the paparazzi were acting completely out of control and causing havoc.

These actions help reveal how thorough the intelligence planning of this operation was. Cowper-Coles and his officers were not just thinking about how to remove the princess – they gave extensive thought into planning for the ensuing cover-up. If the crash could be pinned on other people – the paparazzi, the drunk driver – then that would divert attention away from the true perpetrators.

During the almost three hours from when Diana and Dodi had left the Ritz – at 7 p.m. – and returned – at 9.50 p.m. – MI6 was deeply involved in ensuring all the parts of their master-plan were on track.

Henri Paul, who had earlier stayed around the Ritz as long as Diana and Dodi were there, walked out the front door at 7.01 p.m., exactly four minutes after their departure. He left instructions with the night security manager, François Tendil, to "call me on my mobile phone" if the couple return. He also told Tendil: "They should not be back". This was in keeping with the misinformation that Henri and Roulet were promoting – that the couple would be dining at Chez Benoît. Tendil told the inquest: "They had to go to the restaurant, Chez Benoît".

Where Henri went and what he did over the next three hours has never been explained.

Henri phoned Didier Gamblin, who was on security at Dodi's apartment, at 7.30 p.m. and told him he was "going to leave the hotel and he was going home". This was around half an hour after Henri had already left the hotel. There is evidence indicating Henri never went home – for example, his answering machine wasn't cleared.

Claude Roulet, who was also working for MI6, has claimed that by accident he met with Henri in a bar at around 7.30 p.m. But it has been clearly proved that Roulet was lying – Ritz CCTV shows that Roulet didn't even leave the hotel until 8.20 p.m. and the bar staff said Henri wasn't there.

Henri Paul was not seen by any other witness until 9.45 p.m.

So Henri Paul disappeared for nearly three hours and no witness has come forward to vouch for him. He normally went to dinner at Claude Garrec's every Saturday night, but earlier in the day Henri had told Garrec that he would "not be able to make it tonight. This evening I'll surely be getting off work late."

Henri apparently met with his MI6 handler to receive final instructions and an additional payment. When he died later that night he was carrying FF12,565 – about £1,250.

Henri would not have known his actions would lead to anyone's death – he may have been told there was a special security risk and he was required to do certain things to reduce the danger to Princess Diana.

At 8.15 p.m. Ritz day chauffeur, Olivier Lafaye, drove his Mercedes S280 into the Vendôme car park and left it on the third floor, as he did every evening. He delivered his keys to the board in the foyer and headed home.

Lafaye had no idea that just four hours later his Mercedes would be used to assassinate the famous British princess.

Just five minutes after Lafaye parked the car, at 8.20, Claude Roulet, who had been awaiting Lafaye's return, left the hotel. He met with his MI6 handler and then led him to the Mercedes S280 in the Vendôme car park. A specialist intelligence team had been awaiting this moment and immediately started work on the rear seat belts, ensuring that both were rendered unworkable.

Henri Paul wasn't sighted until about 9.45 p.m. when he visited a local bar, Le Champmeslé. Josiane Le Tellier, the proprietor, later recalled: "He was in the bar for a short while, but did not have a drink. He made an appointment to meet up with friends later that evening at around midnight." Henri had come to pick up his Mini from its regular parking place outside the bar, right near his home. Josiane saw him drive off.

Five minutes later, at 9.50, Diana and Dodi arrived at the front door of the Ritz Hotel. Dourneau, the driver, told the police: "Once we got to the hotel, there was a sea of people". Even though persons directly involved – Dourneau, Delorm and others – had been told the destination was Chez Benoît, it appears that word had somehow got out that the couple were actually going to the Ritz. This increased the pressure of the evening, adding to the tension that had already been building up due to the actions of MI6's fake paparazzi.

Meanwhile, Henri left Le Champmeslé's bar and parked up in his car somewhere along Rue Danielle Casanova, the one way street between his home and the Ritz Hotel. He then sat there waiting for the notification call from the Ritz.

Henri had already been told by his MI6 handler that the couple had left the apartment and he knew the destination was the Ritz. His intelligence job that evening required him to be at the Ritz to ensure the MI6 plans were carried out. He was required to drive the Mercedes S280 for the late-night return trip and there was to be no back-up car.

Henri didn't have to wait long. François Tendil called at 9.59 p.m. and Henri assured him he would "be there straight away". Just seven minutes later, at 10.06, Ritz CCTV cameras recorded him parking his Mini outside the front of the hotel.

PARIS-LONDON CONNECTION

8   Decoy Plan

Henri's first move on entering the Ritz was to locate the English bodyguards, whom he had first met at Le Bourget that afternoon. The head waiter told the police: "He went up to Vincent [the head barman] and asked him where the bodyguards were." Rees-Jones and Wingfield were already in the Bar Vendôme and had ordered dinner. When Henri joined them, two minutes after parking his car, he asked what they wanted to drink. They declined alcohol, but Henri ordered a Ricard for himself.

Henri based himself at the bodyguards' table for the next hour, but the CCTV shows him going in and out of the bar area. He ordered two 5cl Ricards in total – at 45% proof, this would have left Henri Paul's blood alcohol concentration (BAC) under the French safe driving limit of 0.50 g/L at the time the Mercedes S280 left the Ritz Hotel.

Kez Wingfield later lied to the police when he told them: "I thought it was pineapple cordial" Henri was drinking. Trevor Rees-Jones said: "I have absolutely no idea what drink it was." The reason the bodyguards – who are trained to be particularly observant – lied about this was because they were negligent in later allowing Henri to drive the princess, when they both knew he had had a couple of drinks.

Henri may have been told by his MI6 handler to relax – "it's Saturday night" – and have a couple of drinks, to blend in while he waited around. This certainly helped fit the plan MI6 had – to pin the crash on him, as a drunk driver. Even though Henri wasn't over the limit, the fact he did drink later helped investigators to cloud the issue and falsely blame him for the crash.

By the time Diana and Dodi returned to the hotel, at 9.50 p.m., the fake paparazzi pressure had begun to take its toll. Rees-Jones wrote in his book that Diana looked anguished and then was seen crying soon after arriving.

At Le Bourget airport Henri had spoken to Dodi about trusting him and Roulet to address the problem if the paparazzi became too difficult. Then both Roulet and Henri were in the hotel during the 2½ hours between the couple's arrival, at 4.30, and departure, at 7 p.m. They would have had ample time to further discuss the paparazzi situation then – and that was following the horrific ride from Le Bourget to Villa Windsor. It is then that the MI6 late-night decoy plan – use of a third car from the rear entrance – would have been suggested to Dodi, at least as a recommended option. Roulet may have told Dodi to let Henri know if he wanted to proceed with the plan.

After another tense and pressured trip – from the apartment to the hotel – and the "sea of people" on arrival, Dodi had made his mind up: they would go with the decoy plan.

At 10.20 p.m., 30 minutes after arriving back at the Ritz, Dodi told Thierry Rocher, the night manager, to "let Mr Paul know that a third car would be ready in rue Cambon and that they would leave via that exit".

Then nine minutes later, at 10.29, Rocher passed this information on to Henri. Rocher told the police: "When I conveyed this message to Henri Paul he asked no questions whatsoever and seemed to simply accept the instruction."

Henri was expecting the instruction – that's why he had "no questions".

Dodi's message only included aspects of the MI6 decoy plan – it is clear that Dodi was still expecting a back-up car, a professional chauffeur and two bodyguards. MI6 was not. Dodi was told early, by Roulet, about the third car and the rear exit – but not about any details that stripped away the couple's protection.

Rocher later said: Henri "thanked me and said 'I am going to finish my Ricard with the Englishmen'". But that is not what Henri did. Instead, the CCTV shows him exiting the Ritz at 10.34 and walking into the Place Vendôme and out of CCTV range. Henri returns to the hotel nine minutes later, at 10.43 p.m.

He appears to have checked in with his handler who would have been in walking distance of the Ritz. Henri passed on Dodi's acceptance of the decoy plan – even though the plan Dodi accepted was quite different to MI6 intentions.

Dodi, of course, had no idea that the plan came from an intelligence agency – he thought it had been formulated by Claude Roulet, vice-president of the Ritz Hotel.

On re-entering the hotel, Henri immediately rejoined the bodyguards at their Bar Vendôme table. Henri's main purpose in spending so much time with Rees-Jones and Wingfield was to build a rapport. This would soften them up for what was to come – the revelation of the decoy plan. It not only had to be sold to Dodi, but also his bodyguards needed to be on side.

All three, Rees-Jones, Wingfield and Henri, left the bar area at 11.09 p.m. The bodyguards headed upstairs to wait outside the Imperial Suite. Henri again went through the front door of the Ritz, but this time he talked to the paparazzi waiting outside.

Henri was given an additional key responsibility that night. It fell on him to ensure that the waiting paparazzi didn't become discouraged or decide that Diana and Dodi were actually going to stay the night inside the hotel. The paparazzi were a critical component of the MI6 plan – they had to be seen to stay around the Ritz and then leave in pursuit of the couple. Otherwise the whole fake paparazzi pursuit would not be convincing. Henri would have been promised a handsome reward for making sure the paparazzi stayed until Diana and Dodi left.

It is difficult to understand the motives behind Henri's actions on the night. It is possible that he had somehow been falsely led to believe that he was assisting with Diana and Dodi's security. Henri may have been told by MI6 that there was a specific threat to the couple's safety that required unorthodox strategies.

Ritz CCTV shows Henri Paul making four separate visits to talk to the paparazzi out the front of the hotel between 11.10 p.m. and 12.06 a.m. – a period of 56 minutes.

What was he telling them?

Paparazzo, David Odekerken, later told the French police: "He informed us of the countdown regarding the couple's exit. He was speaking to all the journalists. He said 'ten minutes' and then the following time, 'five minutes' and then 'two minutes'."

This was not normal behaviour for security staff at a top-line international hotel. Romuald Rat, another paparazzo who was there, later said: "What shocked me was that he should come and talk to us. At the Ritz, the drivers and doormen must not speak to us and I think that is normal. His attitude was completely the opposite."

Hotel security staff are supposed to protect their guests from the prying eyes of the media. On that night, Henri Paul was doing the opposite – he was freely providing classified information on the couple's movements to the waiting paparazzi. Keeping them interested. Whereas, it was in Diana and Dodi's interests for the waiting media to lose interest and go home – particularly considering the horrific trips the couple had already endured on Paris' streets since their mid-afternoon arrival.

Henri was simply fulfilling a key aspect of his MI6 instructions – making sure the paparazzi stayed on and joined the pursuit. The effect of this would enable the paparazzi to later be blamed for the deaths, even though it was not their actions, but instead the actions of MI6's fake paparazzi that contributed heavily to the crash.

On re-entering the hotel at 11.13, Henri immediately headed upstairs to the Imperial Suite. It is at this point that he proceeded to tell Rees-Jones and Wingfield about the decoy plan. This is the first they have heard of it – just over one hour before departure. Up to this point they believed the couple would be leaving out the front with Dourneau and Musa driving the two cars. The CCTV footage shows a major interaction between Henri, Rees-Jones and Wingfield that goes for five minutes, from 11.14 to 11.19 p.m.

Henri would have had to provide details of the plan to the bodyguards and they were not happy. Henri headed back downstairs at 11.20 and a minute later the CCTV shows Kez Wingfield throwing out his arms, clasping his hands together and slumping forward. Henri's revelation of the decoy plan started a six-minute intense conversation between the two bodyguards.

Rees-Jones and Wingfield have never explained why they accepted a plan with no back-up car. But what is clear is that they were somewhat lax on key rules. Earlier in the day, when the couple were driven to Villa Windsor from the airport, they had allowed the Range Rover to separate from the Mercedes in order to offload at Dodi's apartment. And also, on the nightmarish final trip between the apartment and the hotel – at 9.30 p.m. – the two bodyguards had travelled together in the back-up car. This had left the couple in the Mercedes unprotected if the vehicles had become separated.

Henri should never have been allowed to drive Diana and Dodi – he lacked a Grand Remise chauffeur licence and he also never drove Ritz guests. Rees-Jones and Wingfield were the only people given forewarning – but they were unaware of Henri's background and presumed, or were told, he was a regular driver.

After leaving the bodyguards in a state of shock over the decoy plan, Henri paid his second visit to the paparazzi and then on re-entering the hotel headed straight upstairs to the Imperial Suite again. It is 11.27 p.m.

At 11.30 Henri goes downstairs to take a four minute call from his fellow agent, Claude Roulet. Roulet told the French police that he made the call "to find out how things were going".

Around 11.45 p.m., just over half an hour ahead of Diana and Dodi's departure, Henri paid his third visit to the paparazzi. Meanwhile the bodyguards were escorted by Thierry Rocher to conduct a reconnaissance of the Ritz rear departure area.

The CCTV outside the Imperial Suite shows Henri pacing back and forth, sitting and intermittently talking to Rees-Jones and Wingfield between 11.51 and 12.00. Then, just seconds before Dodi opens the door to tell the bodyguards they will be leaving in a few minutes, Henri had headed back downstairs, this time to the toilet.

This sends Rees-Jones and Wingfield, who don't know where Henri has gone, into a flurry – because Henri is now the main driver. They set about trying to track him down and Rees-Jones enlists the help of François Tendil and Thierry Rocher. But, not even knowing Henri's name, he told them he was looking for "the driver". As far as Tendil and Rocher are concerned, Henri is not the driver, and they go looking for Dourneau and Musa.

In the meantime Henri has left the toilet area and headed out the front door to pay his final visit to the paparazzi. On the way out, he passes Dourneau and Musa who are coming in to report to the bodyguards. They meet with Rees-Jones and Wingfield on the stairs and find out neither of them are the driver being sought. Dourneau recalled the bodyguards telling them, they were looking for the "third chauffeur – the one with the grey hair".

It is 12.04 a.m.

Rees-Jones and Wingfield are becoming distraught and both start heading towards the rear, still looking for Henri. The CCTV then shows they quickly turned around and returned to the suite. At that moment Diana and Dodi exit the Imperial Suite and are met by Wingfield. And Rees-Jones heads downstairs and finally sees Henri coming back in from visiting the paparazzi.

Henri then leads the group – Diana, Dodi and Rees-Jones – to the rear of the hotel. There being no back-up, Wingfield is to stay with the decoy Mercedes out the front.

It is 12.07 a.m. – 16 minutes before the Mercedes S280 crashes in the Alma Tunnel.

At 12.08 Jean-François Musa, who is near his car outside the front of the Ritz, is approached by Claude Roulet. This is the first appearance of Roulet in the vicinity of the hotel since his 8.20 departure, nearly 4 hours earlier. Musa, who owned the company that supplied the Ritz limousines, later told police that Roulet "asked me if I had a vehicle available".

Musa then went into the foyer area, checked the key board and took the keys for the only car available – the Lafaye Mercedes S280. At 12.11 a.m. Musa handed those keys to the Ritz doorman, Sébastien Cavalera, who in turn carried them out to the car jockey, Frédéric Lucard.

While Lucard proceeded to walk to pick up the Mercedes S280 – the third car – from the Vendôme car park, Wingfield spoke with Dourneau and Musa. Wingfield quickly explained the decoy plan and their role – to stay out the front acting as decoys, while Henri drove the VIPs from the rear. This was the first that the drivers had heard about this. Dourneau later recalled: "A bodyguard came to see us in order to get us to put on an act and make out we were leaving: we were to put the headlights on and switch on the engine attracting the paparazzi's attention, while the couple left via the rear."

Henri, Diana, Dodi and Rees-Jones reached the service area at the back of the Ritz at 12.09 – this is at least two minutes before Lucard, the car jockey, received the S280 keys. This meant that Diana and Dodi were left waiting 9 minutes until the third car arrived.

This delay appears to have been because MI6 were waiting to have everything in place – James Andanson in the Fiat Uno, the large bikes ridden by agents.

The trigger on the night for involving the S280 came from MI6 agent, Claude Roulet, when he approached Musa to ask for a car. Roulet was off the premises and had been for nearly four hours. He had been waiting for the "go" signal from his handler, before coming in from the Place Vendôme to talk to Musa. That signal was the sign that everything was organised and ready on the streets of Paris and it was time to set in motion the final chain of events at the Ritz.

This was the method employed by MI6 to control the timing of the crash – the Mercedes S280 sitting in the Vendôme car park was not going anywhere until there was an order to Musa. That order came from Claude Roulet – his part on that night, working for MI6.

After arriving at the rear of the Ritz with the couple, Henri Paul then set about notifying the paparazzi that the departure would actually be from the rear. Between 12.09 and 12.17 a.m., when the S280 arrived at the rear, the CCTV shows Henri exiting the hotel onto Rue Cambon no less than seven times – at 12.09, 12.10, 12.11, 12.12, 12.13, 12.14 and 12.16.

Some of the paparazzi were already waiting outside the rear exit. Jacques Langevin was among them. He later told the police: "I noticed the hotel's head of security standing at the hotel exit in the Rue Cambon, so I thought they were coming out that way." Christian Martinez, who was still around the front, said that Alain Guizard, a colleague positioned at the rear, "telephoned me to tell me that they would be leaving via the rear".

At 12.13 a.m. Henri stepped outside and waved to the paparazzi, who were over the other side of the narrow back lane.

This behaviour was a continuation of the MI6 plan to make absolutely sure that the paparazzi were involved in the pursuit from the hotel – so blame for the crash could be later pinned on them.

Meanwhile Lucard located the S280 and proceeded to drive out of the car park and towards the rear exit. He arrived at 12.17 a.m. – just six minutes before the crash.

Both decoy drivers were sitting in their vehicles out the front, while Henri, Diana, Rees-Jones and Dodi exited the rear and filed down the Rue Cambon, past road works and into the waiting third car.

After entering the Mercedes, Diana and Dodi tried to fasten their seat belts, but found they were both jammed.

PARIS-LONDON CONNECTION

9   Final Journey

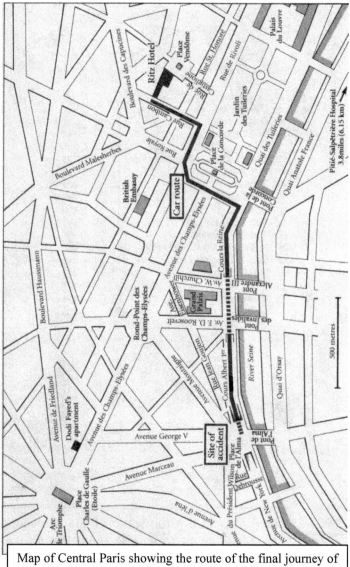

Figure 2   Map of Central Paris showing the route of the final journey of the Mercedes S280 carrying Diana, Princess of Wales, Dodi Fayed, Trevor Rees-Jones and Henri Paul. Original map reproduced from *Death of a Princess: An Investigation*.

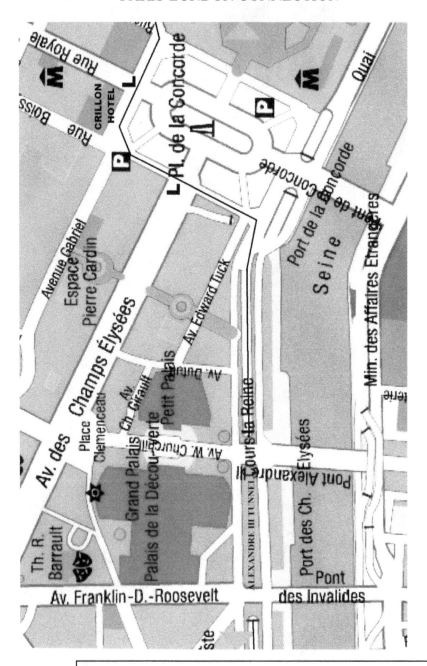

Figure 3

100m

This map shows the route of the Mercedes S280 through the Place de la Concorde, onto the riverside expressway and through the Alexandre III Tunnel. The two sets of traffic lights where the Mercedes stopped are denoted with "L". Original map from Hot Maps: www.hot-maps.de

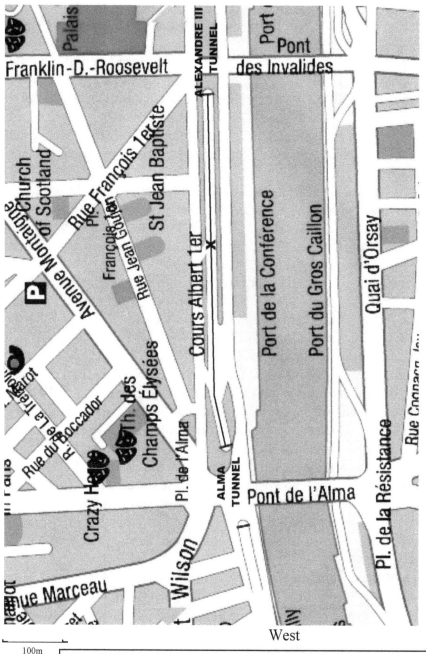

100m

Figure 4 Map showing the route taken by the Mercedes S280 along the riverside expressway, after leaving the Alexandre III Tunnel. The intended exit is marked with an "X". Original map from Hot Maps: www.hot-maps.de

PARIS-LONDON CONNECTION

The S280 departed from the rear of the Ritz Hotel at 12.18 a.m. There was no back-up vehicle.

Henri Paul, who had taken the wheel from Lucard, left at a normal speed and was closely followed by three identified paparazzi vehicles – Alain Guizard driving a Peugeot 205, David Odekerken in a Mitsubishi Pajero and Serge Benhamou riding a Honda scooter.

Frédéric Lucard, who had just vacated the S280's driver's seat, said later that he also saw two unidentified motorbikes following as Henri pulled away.

They headed for Dodi's apartment and by the time the group of vehicles reached Hotel Crillon on the Place de la Concorde they had been joined by Serge Arnal and Christian Martinez, paparazzi who had earlier been outside the front of the Ritz. They were travelling together in Arnal's black Fiat Uno.

Alain Guizard saw the unidentified motorbike riders at the Hotel Crillon traffic lights – "there were three or four of them on two bikes" and the "two motorcycles chased after the Mercedes". These were the same bikes Lucard had seen in Rue Cambon – at least one of them being "a high-powered motorcycle".

Then Guizard saw camera flashes. As with the earlier trips, no photos taken during this important journey have ever been published.

The occupants of the Mercedes noticed that they were again being pursued by paparazzi who wanted to photograph them during the journey. Except these two motorbikes were not paparazzi, but instead were part of MI6's contingent of fake paparazzi.

Serge Benhamou, who was pursuing on his scooter, later described what happened: "The chauffeur slowed down and stopped to let the cars that had a green light go, and then he jumped the lights. He impeded the progress of vehicles that had a green light and they hooted at him."

The Mercedes had to stop again at the Champs Élysées lights. This time it was boxed in. And now the pressure on the occupants intensified considerably.

Another legitimate paparazzo who had been out the front of the Ritz caught up – Romuald Rat riding pillion on Stéphane Darmon's Honda 650.

But it was the MI6 fake paparazzi that were causing the biggest problems for the Mercedes' occupants.

Mohammed Rabouille, a waiting taxi driver, said he saw "several motorcycles behind and near the Mercedes. I thought it was an escort, but there were too many motorcycles for one car".

The windows of the S280 were untinted and this gave any close motorcyclists an unimpeded view inside. Jean-Louis Bonin was in his car sitting in the next lane, level with the Mercedes. He witnessed a pillion passenger between the cars "taking one photograph after another with his flash". Again, these photos have never seen the light of day.

Bonin provided a unique eye-witness account of what was happening inside the S280: "I made out Mr Dodi Al Fayed, whose photograph I had already seen in the newspapers, who had his left hand holding the strap and his right hand shielding his face, which one could make out all the same. To his right I noticed Princess Diana, who was sitting back into her seat to conceal herself. Beside the driver was a fair-haired young man who I realised was the bodyguard. He seemed very annoyed, turning his head a lot, and I guess he wanted the car to move off."

Bonin then described to the police what occurred when the lights changed. "I started off and noticed that the Mercedes was held up by a dark-coloured car which had stopped in front of it."

The French investigators asked Bonin: "Did you get the impression that this car was obstructing the Mercedes deliberately?" Bonin replied: "Definitely."

This was the turning point in the final journey – the realisation by those inside the Mercedes that there could be a sinister element to what was happening. The untoward and constant photographing in transit, being surrounded by motorbikes and now a car deliberately blocking their progress.

This knowledge prompted Henri Paul to react quickly and forcefully. Bonin: "In my interior mirror, I saw the Mercedes which was pulling out and I heard its engine roar loudly and its tyres spin.... Diana's Mercedes overtook me at very high speed on the right." In the words of another witness: "When there was some space in front of them, the Mercedes accelerated radically. It took off just like a plane."

But the Mercedes was not alone.

Thierry Hackett was ahead of the Mercedes on the riverside expressway in the first tunnel, the Alexandre III, when he was overtaken at high speed. Later that day he spoke to the police: The Mercedes "was clearly being chased by several, I would say between four and six, motorcycles. There were two riders on some of the bikes. These motorcycles were sitting on the vehicle's tail and were trying to get alongside it."

Hackett then described what occurred after the group had passed him: "I noticed that the Mercedes was veering from side to side.... Clearly, the driver of the vehicle was being hindered by the motorbikes." And: The Mercedes "was still in the left hand lane. I could still see the light coloured motorcycle at the same level as the Mercedes on the right and the others following."

The motorbike on the right prevented the S280 from leaving the expressway at the only exit before the Alma Tunnel. This was also the exit that had to be taken to get to Dodi's apartment. This unidentified motorcyclist's action left Henri Paul with no alternative – he and his passengers were now headed for the Alma Tunnel, as had been the MI6 plan all along.

François Levistre was travelling with his wife on the parallel service road before entering the expressway just before the Alma Tunnel. He witnessed the group of vehicles as they emerged out of the Alexandre III Tunnel and told police the next day: "I could see in the distance in my rear view mirror a vehicle surrounded on either side by motorbikes. There were more than two motorbikes, travelling in tandem on each side of the car."

US businessman, Brian Anderson, was a passenger in a taxi that was overtaken by the Mercedes and three motorbikes just before the Alma Tunnel. He said: "The bikes were in a cluster, like a swarm around the Mercedes."

Off-duty chauffeur, Clifford Gooroovadoo, was standing in a park near the Alma Tunnel, when he heard the Mercedes approaching. Two hours later he told police that he saw a pillion passenger on a motorbike "taking one photo after another in the direction of the" S280.

Just before entering Paris' Alma Tunnel, the Mercedes S280 carrying Princess Diana and Dodi Fayed was travelling at high speed and surrounded by several MI6-employed motorcyclists – pretending to be paparazzi, but with a clear intent to intimidate or harm those inside. The real paparazzi, driving small cars and riding scooters, were left well behind during this frenzied chase.

On entering the Alma Tunnel, the pressure on the Mercedes' driver and occupants was ratcheted up several notches.

It is now 12.23 a.m. on Sunday 31 August 1997.

Several events – very rapid but pre-planned – are impending.

Within seconds, two men will be murdered, a bodyguard and a princess will be seriously injured.

And as a result, the world would be stunned into silence.

There were traffic cameras along the route, but no footage of the final journey has ever been released.

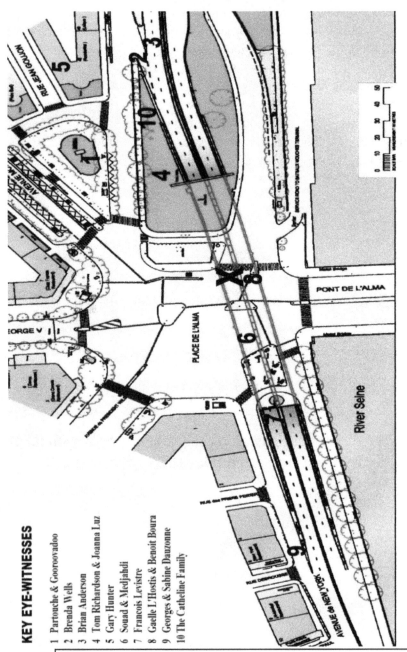

KEY EYE-WITNESSES

1 Partouche & Gooroovadoo
2 Brenda Wells
3 Brian Anderson
4 Tom Richardson & Joanna Luz
5 Gary Hunter
6 Souad & Medjahdi
7 Francois Levistre
8 Gaelle L'Hostis & Benoit Boura
9 Georges & Sabine Dauzonne
10 The Catheline Family

Figure 5 — Map of crash scene showing the positions of the key witnesses at the time of the crash (except the Dauzonnes' position reflects when they witnessed the Fiat Uno post-crash). The crash impact point at the 13th pillar of the Alma Tunnel is denoted with an "X". Witnesses not mentioned in this book are included in the book *Diana Inquest: The Untold Story* (Part 1). Original map produced by the inquest Property Services Dept.

10   In the Tunnel

It is 12.23 a.m., but about 20 seconds before the Mercedes S280 reaches the Alma Tunnel.

David Laurent was driving a Volkswagen Polo. He later described what happened just before entering the tunnel: "I was surprised by a small car, which was driving at an abnormally low speed in the right lane. I do not understand why this car was going so slowly because nothing hampered its progression. It was an old model, light coloured, white or beige, a Fiat Uno type car."

Laurent overtook the white Fiat Uno and continued on through the tunnel. After emerging he heard a "loud crash coming from behind".

Seconds after Laurent passed the Uno the same car was witnessed by Souad Moufakkir, a passenger in her boyfriend Mohammed's car. Just before the crash, the white Uno sped up, then slowed down again.

In Souad's words: "I saw through the back window a Fiat Uno driving very fast up to us, in the outside [left] lane – but rather than hurtle past, it slowed down so we were side by side. It was very strange behaviour, and I got frightened. The white car was only centimetres from ours.... [The driver] had a very strange expression, like his mind was thinking about something else. His whole manner was odd. It troubled me.... I became very scared. I thought he was a madman, and I told Mohammed to speed away. We did that and a moment later we heard the [Mercedes'] screech of tyres."

Forensic analysis of tyre marks later showed that the Uno – which was side-swiped by the Mercedes – was straddling both lanes at the time of impact.

The Fiat Uno was travelling very slow before the tunnel in the right lane, then moved into the left lane and sped up, then abruptly slowed as it drew up beside Souad's car. Then as Mohammed accelerated, the Uno moved in behind to straddle the lanes at the same time it was hit by the S280, just inside the tunnel.

Souad got a good look at the Uno driver – her description was a fit for James Andanson and the white paint left on the Mercedes matched Andanson's model.

Brian Anderson's taxi was overtaken before the tunnel by the Mercedes and at least three motorbikes. Then he observed: "One motorbike proceeded with two people to make a move quickly to the left side of the [Mercedes] and get in front of the automobile."

François Levistre, who was ahead of Souad in the tunnel, told investigators what he saw in his rear-vision: "I saw a motorbike accelerating. It was to the left of a large car that was behind me. The motorcycle, it was large and the two riders had full-face helmets on, cut up the large car in order to get in front of it."

The large, powerful motorbike overtook the Mercedes, which was already in the left lane, on the left – pushing through between the expressway barrier and the car. This occurred at the same time as Henri Paul was just about to enter the tunnel and realised there was a white Fiat Uno straddling the lanes in front of him.

Henri was confronted with a stark, but split-second, choice – either risk hitting the motorbike on his left or the Fiat Uno ahead on his right. Before he could take any action the powerful motorbike was in front of him and the Mercedes side-swiped the Fiat Uno.

The Uno's white paint was left on the Mercedes, but the only person to witness the actual collision was Benoît Boura, who was driving through the tunnel in the opposite direction. He told police: "The Mercedes collided with the first vehicle that was in front of it".

At this precise moment a powerful flash was witnessed by those on the same side as the Mercedes – Brian Anderson, François Levistre and Souad Moufakkir. The flash was from an SAS-issue anti-personnel strobe light carried by the pillion on the motorbike that got in front. He directed it at the driver.

This had the instant effect of blinding Henri Paul. The Mercedes immediately lost control, swinging left and right, then left again, before crashing into the 13th pillar of the Alma Tunnel at about 100 kph.

IN THE TUNNEL

On the huge impact the Mercedes rebounded off the pillar, spinning 180 degrees anti-clockwise, and came to rest facing the tunnel entrance, but diagonally close to the wall.

The crash had made a huge noise and was heard over a wide area.

Many vehicles stopped on both sides of the tunnel and pedestrians and some residents in the general area rushed in.

Other vehicles were witnessed fleeing the crash scene.

11 Fleeing Vehicles

The real paparazzi, who had been left behind in the chase – Rat, Chassery, Guizard, Odekerken, Benhamou, Arnal, Martinez, Darmon – all stopped and stayed around the crash scene.

Other vehicles – including the fake paparazzi – were seen fleeing from the Alma Tunnel.

The white Fiat Uno, which accelerated after the contact with the Mercedes, somehow managed to stay ahead of it, and exited the tunnel.

The motorbike that flashed the Mercedes kept moving, hesitated to survey the scene as it passed and then accelerated quickly out of the tunnel.

A dark Peugeot followed by a white Mercedes passed the crash scene very slowly, assessed the damage and confirmed that there were no movements inside the black Mercedes.

They then both exited the tunnel quickly, together turning right onto Rue Debrousse, then right onto Avenue du President Wilson, across the Place de l'Alma, then both accelerating to speeds in excess of 100 kph along the Rue Jean Goujon.

London lawyer, Gary Hunter, was staying at the Royal Alma Hotel at 35 Rue Jean Goujon. He stated that these two vehicles entered his street a minute or so after he heard the impact noise of the crash and that they were travelling at 60 to 70 mph: "It was obvious that they were getting away from something and that they were in a hurry – it looked quite sinister."

The white Fiat Uno sped up immediately after being hit by the Mercedes. Benoît Boura, who had witnessed the collision between the two vehicles, told the police: "This vehicle accelerated at the time that the Mercedes lost control. I then saw it drive off." His girlfriend, Gaëlle l'Hostis, said it "was never passed by the Mercedes".

The Uno driver, James Andanson, immediately slowed up on hearing and seeing the impact of the crash behind him.

Georges and Sabine Dauzonne, travelling in their Rolls Royce, were about to enter the expressway west of the Alma Tunnel, when they witnessed the emerging white Fiat Uno. Georges said later: "My attention was caught by a vehicle coming out of the tunnel, which was zigzagging and backfiring. The driver didn't see us at all – he was so busy watching what was going on in his inside rear-view mirror and his left hand wing mirror, especially the rear-view. He wasn't paying attention whatsoever to what was happening in front of him. The vehicle almost smashed into us.... I'd thought that either he must be drunk – or that, from the way he was looking in his rear-view mirror, perhaps he was expecting someone to be following him. He was very jumpy."

Georges and Sabine both provided a description of the Uno driver that fitted James Andanson.

Andanson, who has been linked to the premature 1993 death of former French Prime Minister Pierre Bérégovoy, would have been employed by MI6 on a "need to know" basis. His Fiat Uno was used to increase the pressure on the Mercedes driver, but he wouldn't have needed to know that the target was Princess Diana. Andanson may have been very shocked when he discovered the full nature of the operation he had been an integral part of.

The Dauzonnes kept heading west. After passing the white Fiat Uno, Sabine looked back and saw it stopping by the side of the road.

They were the only known witnesses to sight the Fiat Uno outside the Alma Tunnel post-crash.

12 Immediate Aftermath

The Mercedes S280 came to rest inside the Alma Tunnel.

Both the people on the driver's side – Dodi Fayed and Henri Paul – died instantly.

Both the people on the passenger's side – Princess Diana and Trevor Rees-Jones – survived.

Smoke billowed from under the bonnet. The horn was blaring.

Some of the fake paparazzi stopped to take photos.

Radio France trainee reporter, Noe da Silva, was in the tunnel: "There were actually three or four people taking photos of the car with flashes. The photographers were in a circular arc behind the car on the right.... I also saw some motorbikes parked in front of and behind the crashed car."

These photos – as with the photos from the journey – have never been published or offered to the media. Those unidentified motorcyclists then quickly left the tunnel.

A few westbound vehicles continued around the crashed Mercedes.

The true paparazzi arrived – one motorbike, one scooter, three cars – and started taking photos.

Pedestrians took control and prevented cars from entering the tunnel.

Eastbound vehicles were slowing as well and soon almost ground to a halt.

People started phoning the emergency services from mobile phones – some were pedestrians, some were in passing vehicles.

Two minutes after the crash, at 12.25, an experienced Paris emergency doctor, Frédéric Mailliez, arrived in the tunnel. He parked his SOS Médécins car on the other side and went over to the crashed Mercedes.

Pedestrian, Abdelatif Redjil, walked over to Mailliez and "told him that one of the casualties was the Princess of Wales". Yet Mailliez later said he had no idea who it was: "The next day I discovered that the woman I was treating was Princess Diana".

Mailliez is a mystery man.

He arrived in a medical emergency car with a flashing light, but with no medical kit. He called the fire service and directed them to the wrong location. Mailliez told the French police that Diana would not accept an oxygen mask, but later told the media that it helped her to breathe. He said Diana was unconscious when other witnesses said she was talking. In one interview Mailliez said Diana spoke then he retracted that the following day. He says under oath that he worked "for the SAMU" but later said under the same oath "I did not work for the SAMU". He said that the car was his "own vehicle, my own car" then later said the car belonged to SOS Médécins.

It was no coincidence that an emergency doctor was actually passing through the Alma Tunnel at just that time. Dr Mailliez was employed by MI6 to control the immediate post-crash scene. If an emergency doctor was dealing with the patient, Princess Diana, then that effectively prevented anyone else from being able to help her during the critical early minutes. He pretended he never knew it was Diana because that distances him from being a primed agent.

The most consistent factor of Mailliez's accounts over the years has been how inconsistent they are.

When Mailliez attended the scene he quickly assessed there were two dead. But when he decided which of the injured to assist, he went to the least injured – Diana, a person who's "condition did not seem desperate to me", rather than Rees-Jones, who he later described as "alive but severely injured". Given that he denies knowing she was Diana, he has never explained why he did that.

Dr Mailliez was there controlling Diana's situation from 12.25 to 12.32, when the Fire Service, Sapeurs Pompiers, arrived. Those fire officers describe Mailliez leaving the scene just as rapidly as he arrived. Xavier Gourmélon later said: "As soon as we arrived, [Mailliez] presented the situation quickly and then he left". Mark Butt, Mailliez's companion, said: "After the fire services arrived, we quickly left."

This is surprising because Mailliez was a qualified doctor, but he handed Diana over to fire service ambulance officers who were not. Mailliez's primary defence for not treating Diana properly was that he had virtually no equipment, only an oxygen mask – no medical kit. Yet when the equipment arrived, in the form of two ambulances from the fire service, he immediately cleared out.

Mark Butt told the inquest: "A lot of stuff was going on that I did not understand and I was just dealing with it". No one asked Butt to explain what he meant.

In a 1998 interview Mailliez said that after leaving the scene he "decided to take a detour on the way home and drive by the Ritz". This was despite the fact he had hurried away and also his insistence that he was unaware he was treating Princess Diana.

Two passing police officers, Lino Gagliardone and Sébastien Dorzée, arrived at 12.26 a.m. They set about controlling the crash scene.

The earliest eye-witnesses – Abdelatif Redjil, Belkacem Bouzid and Sébastien Dorzée – describe Diana as repeating, "My God. My God".

"I told [Dr Mailliez] that one of the casualties was the Princess of Wales. He replied that she was a casualty like any other."

- Abdelatif Redjil, Pedestrian Eye-Witness, French Investigation Statement, 16 June 1998

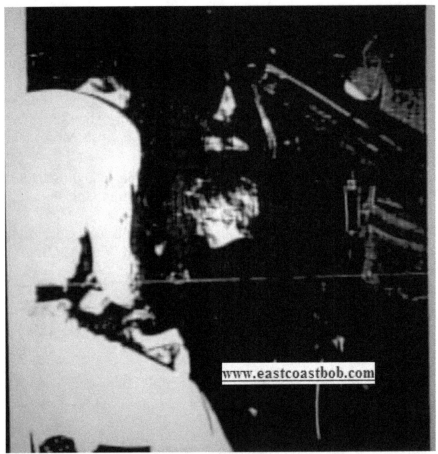

Figure 6

Photo showing Diana conscious, upright and grimacing in the back of the Mercedes, just after the crash. Dr Mailliez is on the left.

13 Early Medical Mistreatment

Two Sapeurs Pompiers – Paris fire service – ambulances arrived at 12.32, nine minutes after the crash. They took medical control of the crash scene until 12.40, when the SAMU ambulance took over.

During those eight minutes of control the two fire service ambulances, which each contained five staff, failed to check Diana's blood pressure.

Fire service officer, Philippe Boyer, was initially assigned to take care of Diana. He later said that they did other basic checks, and "our job was done by then. We had to wait for the physicians from the resuscitation ambulance from the SAMU." It's not that the fire service didn't have doctors. Two of their doctors – Dr Fuilla and Dr Le Hot – arrived at the scene at 12.43, three minutes after the SAMU ambulance.

The orders to the Fire Service were to wait for the SAMU. This is because it was the SAMU doctors – Dr Martino and Dr Derossi – who were operating as MI6 agents on the night.

While they were waiting for the SAMU, the Fire Service medics enlisted one of the policemen – Sébastien Dorzée – to care for Diana. In a report written up that day Dorzée stated that he was told to keep her "as awake as possible, by speaking to her [and] by tapping her cheek".

Within a matter of minutes Diana's primary medical care had been downgraded from a fully-trained emergency doctor – who was in a hurry to get away – to a passing policeman.

In the meantime, SAMU had received notification of the crash by 12.25. Dr Arnaud Derossi was on duty as the medical dispatcher and he took the calls.

A SAMU ambulance with Dr Jean-Marc Martino aboard left at 12.28 a.m. – two minutes before the Fire Service ambulances – but didn't arrive until 12.40 – eight minutes after the Fire Service. The ambulance left from the Necker Hospital which was just 2.3 km from the Alma Tunnel. It took 12 minutes to travel 2.3 km – an average speed of 11½ kph (7 mph). Martino appears to have stopped on the way to receive final instructions from his MI6 handler, because Diana had survived.

One of MI6's key strategies was to delay treatment. Mailliez had expertise but no equipment. The Fire Service had the equipment but was under orders to not send a doctor ahead of SAMU – and to wait until SAMU arrived before administering any treatment to Diana. SAMU delayed their arrival until 12.40 a.m., 17 minutes after the crash.

All this meant that nothing much was done – including no blood pressure test – for Diana until Dr Martino arrived at 12.40 a.m. And Dr Martino was working for MI6, so he also made sure very little was done – in fact Martino's actions were mostly detrimental to Diana's condition. Martino did not treat Diana – he mistreated her.

MI6 had complete control of the medical treatment of Princess Diana, right from 12.25 a.m. when Frédéric Mailliez arrived in the Alma Tunnel, until 2.06 a.m. – when Martino delivered her to the hospital.

On arrival, at 12.40, Martino's team started working with Trevor Rees-Jones, who was assessed as being in the most critical condition. Martino told investigators in 1998: "I asked my crew to take care of the front right hand seat passenger [Rees-Jones], who seemed the more seriously injured of the two, whilst calling for back up from the Mobile Emergency Service [SAMU] in order to attend to the second victim [Diana]."

This decision might sound logical, but it had the effect of further delaying Diana's treatment.

Then at 12.43 the Fire Service's Dr Fuilla arrived. The logical move then would have been for Fuilla's team to treat Diana – because Martino was already working with Rees-Jones.

But that is not what occurred. Instead, Martino's team switched from working on Rees-Jones to Diana – and Fuilla took over the treatment of Rees-Jones.

These decisions enabled Diana's treatment to be delayed another three minutes, whilst Martino – and MI6 officers – were able to still maintain complete control over Diana's treatment.

Xavier Gourmélon, a first aid instructor with the Fire Service, told police that Diana said, "My God, what's happened?"

According to the SAMU ambulance report Diana scored 14 out of 15 on the Glasgow Coma Rating Scale. Tom Treasure, the inquest cardio-thoracic expert, later said: "14 out of 15 is very good.... It is a scale of prediction of head injury and it was very favourable." This is further medical evidence contradicting Mailliez's account that Diana was unconscious.

It was however obvious to the medical people attending the crash scene that Diana had been involved in a very serious high-speed crash impact – and hadn't been wearing a seat belt.

Dr Mailliez later said: "I was just suspecting a brain damage or a chest damage because of the high-energy accident." Dr Martino also made an early assessment: "Because of what happened at the scene, that is to say a high-speed accident, the technical wherewithal capable of operating in thoracic, cardiac and abdominal regions was needed."

In other words, it was evident from the beginning that, although Diana looked okay on the outside, there would be some internal damage from having been involved in this violent crash.

This then meant that Martino understood Diana required treatment in a hospital – a place with "the technical wherewithal capable of operating".

From that point on – soon after arriving at 12.40 – Martino, had he been interested in saving Diana, would have been trying to get her to a hospital as soon as possible. Yet that is not what occurred – Diana didn't arrive at La Pitié-Salpêtrière Hospital until 2.06 a.m.

It took Martino 1 hour 26 minutes to deliver her to a hospital. Then she died six minutes after arriving.

It is a shocking story.

Dr Arnaud Derossi, who was operating the phones at SAMU base, took the initial notification calls and dispatched Martino's ambulance to the scene. He also operated as an MI6 agent on the night. Derossi's SAMU colleague, Dr Marc Lejay, was asleep at the time of the crash. He was not involved with MI6.

Derossi woke Lejay, who then took over as medical dispatcher – and Derossi left SAMU control in his car at 12.42, arriving at the crash scene eight minutes later, at 12.50. Just like Martino, he also probably spoke with his MI6 handler along the way.

At 12.43 Martino called Lejay with a situation report: "Rear passenger, would seem an arm, the right arm, completely turned backwards. We are trying to sedate and initial treatment. Over." That rear passenger was Princess Diana.

Martino, however, later told French investigators that his initial assessment was much more than that: "She herself had a facial injury, frontal according to the journey log, and was trapped with her right arm bent to the rear, at first glance possibly with a fracture in the upper third. However, she may have had all sorts of other internal injuries, abdominal or thoracic, which might decompensate at any time."

The idea behind calling base with assessments is so the receiving hospital can be chosen and preparations made to have the right staff – doctors and specialists – available on arrival. This is particularly the case for a VIP, as Princess Diana was.

Dr Martino failed to inform the base of his initial assessment that Diana had a facial injury and could be expected to have "internal injuries, abdominal or thoracic". Instead he lied, and only told Lejay about a likely arm injury.

He mentioned an injured arm but omitted potentially life-threatening internal injuries.

This was good news for the SAMU base. They had a crash involving a British princess on their hands, but the only injury was to her arm.

It meant there was no need to rush Diana to hospital and there was no expected requirement to have any particular specialists on hand.

But even more important, it reduced the pressure on Martino – it meant he would not have the base breathing down his neck and it strengthened his independent control of the scene. SAMU were in charge of Diana and Martino was their doctor on the spot. And Dr Derossi was on his way. Both were agents of MI6.

It is no coincidence that Martino's "injured arm" report is sent in just after Derossi had left. It is unusual for a dispatcher to go to the scene and if it had been "known" that Diana only had an injured arm, his trip would have seemed unnecessary. Derossi would have notified Martino he had already left before Martino called in with the report. Martino would need Derossi at the crash scene.

Martino left Diana in the back of the Mercedes for another 17 minutes, removing her at 1 a.m. and she was in the ambulance by 1.06. But by that time Martino had her anaesthetised, intubated and ventilated.

A patient is much easier to control if they are unconscious and unable to talk. Intubation and ventilation is an extreme process. It involved placing a flexible plastic tube down Diana's windpipe. For this to occur, Diana had to be anaesthetised. These procedures are only carried out prior to hospital if it is absolutely necessary.

In Diana's case it was not.

After Marc Lejay was told about this treatment at 1.19 a.m. he said to Derossi that it "was rather strong for the circumstances". The inquest expert, Professor Tom Treasure, said that in the UK ambulance crews don't intubate unless the person is so incapacitated that it can be done without the use of drugs. He also stated that anaesthetising the patient makes them "much harder to analyse in terms of their brain injury and so on".

So it is a last resort.

Diana was not a last resort patient. She had a Glasgow coma rating of 14 out of 15 and was not having trouble with breathing.

On arrival at 12.50 Derossi joined Martino's ambulance crew, bringing the number on board to five – Jean-Marc Martino, Arnaud Derossi, Barbara Kapfer, a person called "Fadi", and the driver, Michel Massebeuf. The inquest jury were only informed of three – Martino, Massebeuf and an unnamed "medical student".

Once inside his ambulance Martino undressed and examined the now unconscious Diana.

The first page of the ambulance report reveals the results of that examination under the heading "Findings". Right arm and right leg injuries are mentioned and also "thoracic trauma".

So by 1.15 a.m. Martino is aware that Diana has a thoracic trauma – and by his own later admission to the medical investigators that indicates an "internal injury" in that area. This in turn confirmed the requirement to get Diana to a place with, in his words, "the technical wherewithal capable of operating in thoracic" – a hospital.

But that is not what occurred. In fact, the opposite occurred.

At 1.19 Dr Derossi, who is now in the ambulance, phoned through a report to Dr Lejay. He told Lejay two critical lies. He said Diana had "obvious cranial trauma" and he also stated, "at first appearance, nothing to report for the thorax". And then Derossi repeated "nothing for the thorax" later in the conversation.

Martino's examination revealed the area where a life-threatening internal injury could lie – the thorax – yet Derossi told Lejay "nothing for the thorax" twice. But also said, "obvious cranial trauma" – something which is not in the record of Martino's examination.

The effect of this information for Lejay would be that when calling the hospital he would definitely not be asking for a cardio-thoracic specialist to be on hand, but instead would be seeking the presence of a head trauma specialist.

Martino also wrote that Diana's blood pressure had dropped but failed to record the level. Derossi told the base that it was 70. When Lejay heard this, he suggested the low blood pressure might be due to the sedatives Martino had administered – Lejay described them as "a bit violent" for the circumstances. Martino had administered Fentanyl, which is over 80 times more powerful than morphine.

During later cross-examination at the inquest, Martino admitted that 70 is not actually that low. He was asked: "What is your definition of 'stability'" at a crash scene? Martino answered: "Blood pressure between 60 and – a minimum of 70 to 80 units of arterial blood pressure".

Now in the ambulance, Martino proceeded to use the "low" blood pressure as a pretext to start pumping catecholamines into Diana's system – right from about 1.10 through to 2.06 a.m., when she was delivered to the hospital.

The effect of catecholamines is that it increases the blood pressure, but it also increases the pressure on any potential internal injury. So it should only be administered if absolutely necessary.

In Diana's case catecholamines were not necessary because her blood pressure was not that low, but even more important, the thoracic trauma had revealed the likelihood of an internal chest injury. This meant that the application of catecholamines could be detrimental to Diana's condition.

And Dr Martino – being a doctor – would have definitely been aware of that.

At the inquest, expert Tom Treasure criticised Martino's actions: "Struggling to get a perfect pulse and blood pressure may be wrong; you want one that is just good enough..... The [catecholamines] being counterproductive, they are flogging the heart, they are tightening the circulation. But the real problem is the hole in the blood vessel and, if anything, you are making ... things worse."

Diana had a critical torn vein and the thoracic trauma should have told Martino that such an internal injury was likely.

By pouring in catecholamines Martino was ensuring that any internal injury would be made worse and in turn would help bring on Diana's death.

Dr Martino told the inquest that a blood pressure of 70 and a pulse of 100 – which Diana had at 1.10 – was stable. Yet he failed to move the ambulance out of the tunnel until 1.41 – 31 minutes later.

During the 1.19 report Lejay, at the base, asked whether the ambulance was "ready to roll". He was told by Derossi that it would leave in "a few minutes". Then 10 minutes later, at 1.29 a.m., Lejay calls the ambulance and asks if they are "en route yet". This is even though Lejay was unaware of the thoracic trauma. Had he been told about that, he would have been even more keen for the ambulance to get to the hospital quickly.

A key French defence is that things are done differently there – that ambulances linger longer at the scene: it is called "stay and play". That is true, to a point. But the questions from Lejay, wanting the ambulance to get moving, and the obvious fact that Diana's condition required early hospitalisation, overwhelm any stay and play argument. The requirement for hospitalisation was even admitted by Martino in his early assessment to the French investigators.

Drs Martino and Derossi deliberately lingered as long as they could in the Alma Tunnel, while they simultaneously pumped catecholamines into Diana, knowing that was harmful to her. And they also withheld knowledge of a thoracic trauma from the SAMU base.

The ambulance finally trundled out of the tunnel at 1.41 a.m., followed by two French journalists – Pierre Suu and Thierry Orban.

It was 1 hour and 18 minutes since the crash.

There were six people on board – Princess Diana, Jean-Marc Martino, Barbara Kapfer, and "Fadi" were in the back and Arnaud Derossi and driver, Michel Massebeuf, were in the front.

The destination hospital was La Pitié Salpêtrière.

Normally the procedure was for the SAMU base to determine the hospital. That did not happen in this case. Instead, during the 1.19 call, Derossi specifically told Lejay to book Diana in to "the neurosurgical unit at the Pitié-Salpêtrière Hospital". The reason Derossi did this was apparently because he had been told there was no cardio-thoracic specialist on duty there that night.

There was a hospital where VIPs and political leaders were always sent to, which did have all the specialists on duty 24 hours for emergencies. That was the Val de Grâce. It was just 4.6 km from the crash scene, whereas La Pitié was 5.7 km. In the early edition of *The People* published on the day of the crash, it said that Diana was "believed to be in the French VIP Val de Grâce hospital in central Paris".

That was the logical hospital.

A French emergency physician was later quoted: "Every political figure who is in a car crash or is injured is taken there.... The Val de Grâce ... has a top team of trauma specialists on duty around the clock. I might have helicoptered her in. She would have been on the operating block a few minutes after being stabilised."

But it was not in the MI6 plan for Diana to be properly treated for her injuries – in fact, the plan was that she wouldn't survive that night – and part of that was sending her to the wrong hospital.

Pierre Suu, who followed the ambulance from the tunnel, said it was "being driven at walking pace". The ambulance travelled at an average speed of 17 kph (11 mph) then at 2 a.m. was seen to stop for five minutes within 500 metres of the hospital.

Suu later told the police that "a doctor jumped out of the passenger side of the vehicle and rushed round the back of the ambulance and got inside". That doctor was Arnaud Derossi.

Thierry Orban, who was near Suu, said the ambulance "was rocking".

Martino said he stopped the ambulance because Diana's blood pressure had dropped and he "increased the quantity of the drip volume". He specifically told the police: "I did not do any cardiac massage at that moment".

Martino has never said what level Diana's blood pressure fell to. His explanation for the stoppage of the ambulance does not account for Derossi's sudden move from the front to the back, or the rocking ambulance.

It seems likely that some procedure was carried out during the five minute stoppage that helped quicken Diana's death.

The ambulance started moving again at 2.05 and arrived at the hospital at 2.06.

There was no cardio-thoracic specialist on hand. Instead, he was asleep at home. Dr Alain Pavie, the cardio-thoracic specialist, was phoned at 2.10 a.m., four minutes after Diana arrived.

Two minutes later Diana stopped breathing on the operating table. She never regained her breath.

Princess Diana passed away six minutes after being delivered to hospital – and two minutes after the cardio-thoracic specialist had been called.

It was 2.12 a.m.

The La Pitié medical team, led by Dr Bruno Riou, did the best they could, but in the circumstances they had no chance of saving Diana.

That is because the actions of Drs Martino and Derossi had already sealed her fate. Effectively those two doctors had assassinated Princess Diana in the back of their ambulance, on the orders of their MI6 handlers. They would have been generously remunerated for their actions.

Riou and his team worked feverishly away for a further two hours in a desperate but hopeless attempt to save a princess who was already dead.

They officially gave up at 4 a.m. – 3 hours and 37 minutes after the crash in the Alma Tunnel.

"[Diana's] death stunned me all the more as I was able to get a look at the particulars of the autopsy findings very soon after her death.... She died of internal bleeding. The injury which caused the bleeding was to a vein which doesn't bleed particularly quickly – in fact, it bleeds rather slowly.... If Princess Diana had been brought to hospital within 10 minutes of the accident ... she could have survived."

- Prof Christiaan Barnard, Prominent South African Heart Specialist

"With this type of injury, time is of the essence.... In the United States the delay in getting [Diana] to the hospital could constitute gross malpractice. There's no excuse for it."

- Dr Michael Baden, Chief Forensic Pathologist for New York State Police

"Given that [Diana] was still alive after nearly two hours, if they'd have gotten her [to the hospital] in an hour, they might have saved her."

- Dr John Ochsner, US Cardio-Vascular Surgeon

"If they had gotten [Diana] to the emergency room sooner, she would have had a far greater chance. You could never diagnose that kind of injury in the field, never.... Spending all that time on on-site treatment was absolutely the wrong approach for this patient."

- Dr David Wasserman, US Emergency Room Doctor

"We believe that you have a 'golden hour' to save someone's life.... As soon as you get to the casualty, you stabilise them, then you move them as fast as possible, often by helicopter, to a centre where you can perform surgery.... If [Diana] had had that done, most of us [cardiologists] think she probably would have lived."

- Dr Stephen Ramee, A Leading New Orleans Cardiologist

PARIS-LONDON CONNECTION

14 French Fraud

Professor Bruno Riou, the senior doctor on duty at La Pitié Hospital, had suspicions about the actions of the ambulance doctors.

He was on duty that night and took a call at 1.25 a.m. from Marc Lejay advising him to expect victims from a crash in a tunnel. It wasn't until 1.55 that he learned one of those victims was Princess Diana.

Then, when the VIP patient finally arrived, she was only minutes away from death.

The first action by Riou was to take X-rays of Diana's chest and pelvic area. These revealed the impact of the thoracic trauma and it is at that point that he called for the cardio-thoracic specialist, Dr Alain Pavie.

Riou would have been asking why he wasn't told earlier about the thoracic trauma and also why it took 1¾ hours to get Diana to hospital.

These issues aroused suspicion for Riou, who had 12 years' experience as a doctor.

Minutes after Diana had officially died he completed her death certificate and ticked "yes" for "suspicious death" – and then at about 4.30 he faxed that form off to the Public Prosecutor's Office.

Maud Coujard, the on call deputy Public Prosecutor for Paris, had arrived at the scene around 12.50, just 27 minutes after the crash.

Once there, she was ambushed by the two most senior police officials in Paris – Patrick Riou, head of the Judicial Police and Philippe Massoni, the Paris Prefect of Police. Coujard believed it was a car accident and was expecting to simply appoint the BCA[4] to run the

---

[4] Bureau Central des Accidents – Central Accident Bureau of the French police.

French investigation. She would quickly find out that Riou and Massoni had other plans. They had decided, possibly before the crash occurred, that the investigation would be handled by the Brigade Criminelle, even though that organisation had never before investigated a car crash. The Brigade normally handled murders, kidnappings and terrorism.

Riou even knew which officer he wanted to head the investigation – Jean-Claude Mulès, a person he knew to be corrupt or corruptible, who would assist in reaching the desired investigative conclusion: a tragic accident.

Coujard put up a fight, but she was a lowly official and was steam-rolled by the combination of Riou and Massoni. In desperation, Coujard phoned her boss, Public Prosecutor Gabriel Bestard, in the middle of the night. They then reached a compromise – the investigation would be jointly conducted between the Brigade Criminelle and the BCA.

What actually happened though was the BCA, which had already commenced its inquiries, was completely removed from the investigation that day – and it was instead fully carried out by the Brigade Criminelle, acting alone. The investigator put in charge was Jean-Claude Mulès. Mulès later said: "The director of the judicial police [Patrick Riou] asked me and appointed me". In making this appointment, Patrick Riou bypassed the head of the Brigade Criminelle, Martine Monteil.

The BCA investigators who initially attended the scene and were then removed from the investigation wrote in their report: "The BCA were told that the Brigade Criminelle would be completing the full description and investigation of the scene". BCA investigator, Thierry Brunet, told the inquest: "I have been put aside from this procedure and it was the Criminal Brigade which was involved".

Maud Coujard stayed at the crash scene until about 3.30 a.m., and then returned home. Shortly after 4.00 she received a phone call telling her of the death of Princess Diana. She notified her boss, Gabriel Bestard, then soon after that received a copy of the faxed death certificate completed by Dr Bruno Riou. Coujard took note that Riou had ticked "suspicious death" and quickly arranged to meet with Bestard.

It is not normal to conduct autopsies on road accident passengers, but throughout this particular Sunday, the bodies of Princess Diana and

Dodi Fayed would both be subjected to two autopsies – one in Paris and the second in London.

Coujard and Bestard met before 4.45 and discussed the ramifications of the "suspicious death" direction on Diana's death certificate. They decided that an autopsy had to be conducted on both bodies, otherwise the media would be asking why Diana and not Dodi.

At 4.45 a.m. Maud Coujard called Professor Dominique Lecomte.

Dominique Lecomte, head of the Paris IML[5], had a big day ahead of her.

Being a pathologist, dead bodies were her business and she had three very important ones to deal with that day. None of it could be delegated because she was being rewarded handsomely to fudge the results. But not from the IML. She was also working as an agent for intelligence, either DGSE or MI6.

Her first job was to do a quick autopsy on the body of Diana, Princess of Wales – at the La Pitié Salpêtrière Hospital. Lecomte was working on instructions from the Public Prosecutor's office, but after contacting her intelligence handler, had additional orders from them.

She was in the hospital by 5.15 a.m. – just 1¼ hours after Diana's official time of death. Lecomte had a short meeting with the two senior doctors involved, Bruno Riou and Alain Pavie. Riou aired his suspicions and his reasons. Then she was ready to commence the Diana autopsy at 5.30.

She was not alone. The head of the investigation, Jean-Claude Mulès, was present. Martine Monteil, the Brigade Criminelle head, later stated to British police: "I then had to dispatch a team of officers" to the Diana autopsy. Other than Mulès, these police officers were never identified.

Photos were taken. Mulès later told British police that he had them developed and "handed them personally to Monteil who he saw place them into her office safe".

Coujard – who was not a party to the conspiracy – had asked Lecomte to determine cause of death. The instructions relayed through

---

[5] L'Institut Médico-Legal de Paris – the Paris Institute of Forensic Medicine.

MI6 were to take samples, including blood and urine, that could determine pregnancy.

The autopsy process lasted 50 minutes, finishing at 6.20. It was while this autopsy was taking place – at 6.09 a.m. Paris time – that the Queen announced to the world that she was "deeply shocked and distressed by this terrible news".

Lecomte's busy morning continued. She packed up her equipment and left the hospital, heading for much more familiar territory – her office at the IML. Once there, she organised the testing of the samples and wrote up Diana's autopsy report – cause of death was "internal haemorrhaging" and a "wound to the left pulmonary vein".

At 6.45 a.m. Lecomte teamed up again with Mulès to conduct the Dodi autopsy. This time there was no pressure – it was only carried out to match the treatment of Diana's body. It was quickly wrapped up in 30 minutes, concluding at 7.15.

But the big one, from Lecomte's point of view, was still to come.

During the course of the morning Lecomte had received a request from the Prosecutor's office to conduct an autopsy on the driver, Henri Paul. This was standard procedure – in any fatal car crash samples from the driver had to be taken.

The plan to pin the crash on a drunk driver had been formulated by MI6 well before the crash occurred. It is likely that Lecomte was told ahead of time that she would be required to find a body, from within the IML, with a high level of intoxication. Samples from that second body would need to be used to "establish" Henri Paul's level of intoxication.

Lecomte – who the previous year had conducted a fraudulent autopsy on the body of Judge Bernard Borrel – would have been rewarded handsomely for her actions. She was told what was needed. It was up to her to establish how this was done within the framework of the IML. Because she was the boss it was easier for her to cover up for her illegal activities.

It was at this point that Lecomte appears to have made a critical error of judgement.

There were 25 bodies in the mortuary at the time of the driver's autopsy. Lecomte had to choose a second body with a BAC[6] well over the French drink drive limit. In making her choice she picked a person

---

[6] Blood Alcohol Concentration.

who was heavily intoxicated, but they had died as a result of asphyxiation in a fire. Tests would later reveal that the body had a high BAC with an extremely high level of carbon monoxide – indicating the person would have been unable to walk at their time of death. This in turn created a headache for the authorities determined to blame Henri Paul for the crash – because he was walking with ease as he slipped into the driver's seat of the Mercedes outside the Ritz Hotel.

By 8.20 a.m. both bodies were in the autopsy room and Lecomte commenced work – assisted by none other than Jean-Claude Mulès. Mulès later told the British police that he believed "a decision was made at a high level" to have him assist Lecomte. Also present was an IML assistant, Yves Andrieu, and an unidentified police photographer.

Lecomte took a full set of samples – including several of blood – from both bodies. The samples from the second body were set aside for toxicology testing, whereas Henri Paul's samples were kept separate and later were used to "prove" the DNA of the tested samples.

There was actually no proper identification procedure for either body, with Jean-Claude Mulès claiming he was able to identify Henri Paul because he had viewed him at the crash scene.

At one stage during the autopsy a photo was taken of blood samples next to Henri Paul's body – yet his body hadn't yet been opened up. Those samples had been taken from the second body.

Two sets of documents were drawn up with the name "Henri Paul" assigned to both. The documents however showed up differences in both body weight and height.

Then, when Lecomte drew up her official autopsy report for Henri Paul the following day, she mistakenly included measurements from the second body.

Both sets of samples remained in the IML storage overnight. Early the following morning – Monday September 1 – the police toxicology department was provided with a blood sample from the second body, labelled "XM", meaning "unknown male". That sample was tested by police toxicologist Ivan Ricordel before 10 a.m. and produced a BAC result of 1.87 – over three times the French legal alcohol limit.

Events moved quickly.

At 11.38 the Public Prosecutor's office sent off a fax to Paris toxicologist, Gilbert Pépin, requesting him to carry out a BAC test on a second Henri Paul blood sample. Pépin later claimed to the British investigation that his laboratory, ToxLab, was "responsible for all toxicological analysis from the IML in Paris".

As with Lecomte, Pépin too was on the take from French or British intelligence.

ToxLab picked up a second blood sample from the IML – again from the batch taken from the second body. By 1.19 p.m. Pépin had this tested and quickly got a result similar to Ricordel's – 1.74 and again over three times the French legal limit.

Pépin reported his finding to the Public Prosecutor.

That afternoon the Public Prosecutor's office went public with the BAC findings, publishing a press release. The news was subsequently splashed around the world – the driver of Princess Diana's death car, Henri Paul, was driving drunk, three times over the French limit.

This, despite the fact that the findings were based on a fraudulent Lecomte autopsy and the blood tested came from a body other than Henri Paul's.

At 3.37 p.m. Pépin set about conducting unauthorised and illegal toxicological testing on the blood sample in his possession. His apparent aim was to establish, ahead of time, if there were going to be any shocks in the toxicology of the second body's sample. The carbon monoxide tested extremely high – from that point on the authorities learned there was a major problem that had to be dealt with: How to explain extremely high BAC and carbon monoxide in a person who was walking around soberly in the hotel prior to the Mercedes' departure.

The following day, Tuesday September 2, a corrupt judge, Hervé Stéphan, was appointed to head the French judicial investigation into the crash.

On Wednesday the 3rd a police search of Henri Paul's flat uncovered very little alcohol – just one unopened bottle of champagne and quarter of a bottle of Martini.

Stéphan then officially requested Pépin to conduct toxicological testing on Henri Paul's samples.

Meanwhile a plan was devised between Pépin, Lecomte and Stéphan to deal with the carbon monoxide issue. A leading UK pathologist, Peter Vanezis, had already arrived in Paris on September 2, and was starting to ask awkward questions about the Lecomte autopsy. The three realised that at some stage the very high level of carbon monoxide would become known to other independent experts. It was decided to wait as long as practicable and then hold a second autopsy, this time only on the second body – there would be no need for Henri Paul's body to be there. Pépin knew that carbon monoxide levels in dead bodies decrease over time. This time the autopsy would be carried out by a different pathologist and the sample would be taken from the femoral area – that would also help produce a lower carbon monoxide level. On top of this, they decided to produce "evidence" showing that the blood in Lecomte's autopsy had been taken from the unreliable chest cavity area, rather than the heart. This would have the effect of undermining the importance of the first autopsy – with the high carbon monoxide level – and instead leave the second autopsy as the "reliable" one.

The three people – Lecomte, Stéphan and Pépin – all knew what they had to do and set about carrying this plan out.

Stéphan officially called for the second autopsy on September 4 – he later told British police it was "something that I had never done before". He visited the IML at 5 p.m. and the autopsy was conducted by Dr Jean-Pierre Campana. There was a police photographer present, but the photos have never been seen by anyone who knew what Henri Paul looked like. And this time there was no identification of the body.

Not one of the people present was heard from at the inquest.

Earlier in the day ToxLab had picked up the remaining IML samples from the second body in the first autopsy, and Pépin had carried out the toxicology tests on those. The carbon monoxide level was similar to what he had found in his unauthorised illegal test on September 1, 20.7%.

After that, in a most unusual development, Gilbert Pépin attended the second autopsy. Stéphan later said: "M. Gilbert Pépin ... accompanied me there". It is not normal for a toxicologist to attend an autopsy – and it is even less normal for him to arrive there in the company of the investigating judge. Pépin and Stéphan would have been desperate for the pathologist to carry out the sampling in such a way as to secure a much lower carbon monoxide level. Pépin told the British police: "It was decided at my request to take a sample of blood from the femoral vein".

Pépin collected one of the two blood samples taken and took it straight back to the ToxLab laboratory. The following morning, Friday September 5, he carried out toxicology tests on the sample, but didn't declare one for carbon monoxide.

The UK pathologist, Peter Vanezis, who had been asking questions, returned home that day. The French did not tell him they had carried out a second autopsy.

After further discussions between Stéphan, Lecomte and Pépin over that weekend, Stéphan sent a formal request on the Monday to Lecomte asking her to clarify the sample source in her first autopsy. As they had already planned, she replied on Tuesday the 9th saying the blood samples had come from the "left haemothorax area" – the unreliable and contaminated chest cavity area.

In one fell swoop this would undermine the extreme carbon monoxide level findings from the Lecomte autopsy.

September 9th turned out to be a busy day for Dr Pépin. He finally produced his official results from the first autopsy testing – four days late. This included the 20.7% carbon monoxide level. It was now safe for Pépin to produce that figure, because he already knew that Lecomte was effectively destroying its credibility with her reply to Stéphan. And as well, he now had a much more acceptable carbon monoxide result from the second autopsy.

Pépin simultaneously produced his second autopsy report, including the new carbon monoxide result – 12.8%.

Meanwhile on the same day the French police carried out a second search of Henri Paul's flat. This time they were much more "successful" – they "uncovered" 18 separate bottles containing alcohol, the full range of beer, wine, spirits and aperitifs. Just six days earlier they had found only 1¼ bottles.

Henri Paul's friend, Claude Garrec, was present during the second search. He said later that the police "wrote down the names of alcoholic drinks they claimed they had found, but were not there". Henri's housekeeper, Sandra Cudelo, had already told police on the day before the search: "Henri Paul mostly drank Diet Coke and mineral water."

The "case" against Henri Paul was growing stronger by the day!

Now there were two fraudulent autopsies and a corrupt police search.

Once Stéphan had the written admission from Lecomte that the first autopsy samples were from contaminated blood, he had to work out how to handle it.

This particularly became an issue in March 1998, when the Al Fayed experts were provided access to the French investigation dossier. If he made it available to them at that stage, then the Lecomte autopsy would have immediately lost credibility. Although Stéphan was happy to see that happen, it was not in French interests for it to occur too rapidly.

He decided to initially keep the September 9 Lecomte document, reference D1164, out of the dossier. Then later the document was put back in but not in the right place. It was buried by Stéphan and it wasn't until 2006 that the British police "discovered" it – by then it was 9 years after the crash and the sensitivity over the validity of the first autopsy was greatly diminished. This then enabled both the British police investigation and the inquest to suggest that the huge carbon monoxide level was a mystery, but anyway it came from contaminated blood, so it was not significant.

Nothing could be further from the truth. Early documentation reveals that Lecomte took the first autopsy tested samples from the heart blood of the second body.

As if Stéphan had not done enough to besmirch the name of Henri Paul, on September 11 he ordered Pépin and a Bordeaux toxicologist, Dr Véronique Dumestre-Toulet, to organise CDT[7] testing on the blood samples. CDT can assist in determining alcohol consumption habits of people.

Dumestre-Toulet produced a CDT result that indicated "moderate chronic alcoholism for at least a week". However Dumestre-Toulet's test was conducted on September 10 – the day before the order from Stéphan. And it was taken on a sample that was neither from Henri Paul nor the second body – no sample was ever sent from Paris to her Bordeaux laboratory.

Dr Pépin never volunteered the 20.7% carbon monoxide level to the UK experts. But on 12 November 1997 experts working for Mohamed Al Fayed discovered it during a meeting with French lawyers. Forensic

---

[7] Carbohydrate-Deficient Transferrin.

toxicologist, Professor John Oliver, later wrote: "Although levels were measured in the laboratory, no mention of these levels appeared in the toxicology details presented."

After that, in December, Oliver and Vanezis requested a meeting with Lecomte and Pépin, but that was refused.

Feeling under pressure, in June 1998 Judge Stéphan appointed Lecomte and Pépin to carry out an investigation into the high carbon monoxide levels. On October 16 Lecomte and Pépin reported back, stating that they "logically established" that the high carbon monoxide came from the airbags in the car. This was despite Mercedes Benz stating that the Mercedes S280 airbags contain minimal amounts of carbon monoxide. An earlier test of Dodi Fayed's blood had revealed a carbon monoxide level of under 5%, which is normal.

Lecomte and Pépin had clearly fudged their report and it was rejected out of hand by the UK experts. In February 1999 they made an application for a judicial "confrontation" with Lecomte and Pépin, to discuss the elevated carbon monoxide. But this was also refused.

In the end, the 9 September 1997 report from Lecomte surfaced during the later British police investigation. From that point on – including right through the inquest – that document was used to falsely show that the first autopsy samples were contaminated. And in turn, the second autopsy was more reliable.

The truth is that the samples tested from both autopsies were taken from the second body. The carbon monoxide result of 20.7% was true because it was from smoke inhalation in the body of a fire victim – not Henri Paul.

In embracing the fraudulent second autopsy, the UK police and inquest investigators argued that the associated 12.8% carbon monoxide level must have been a result of Henri Paul's smoking. Of course that is impossible because the samples weren't from Henri Paul.

But even that argument's logic didn't stack up. Henri Paul did smoke cigars and that would have increased his carbon monoxide level – but not to anywhere near 12.8%. Tests have shown that only 1 in 175 smokers could attain that level and Henri was not even a chain smoker.

This was another example of investigators clutching at straws in a desperate attempt to cover up the truth.

In 1999 Judge Hervé Stéphan concluded the French investigation. He "found" that the deaths of Princess Diana and Dodi Fayed had been caused by a drunk driver, Henri Paul.

Henri Paul's actual samples were never officially toxicology tested, but were later used to confirm his DNA.

The samples from the second body were used for the toxicology testing, and they were never DNA tested. In May 2006 Gilbert Pépin told British investigators that they never would be. He said: "The Queen of England would have to negotiate with the President of France for this to be done."

There was never any evidence heard from Dominique Lecomte and Gilbert Pépin at the London inquest.

15 French Response

The initial BCA investigators arrived at the crash scene at 12.53 a.m., just 30 minutes after the crash. They were surprised to find the top police officers in the country were already there.

Philippe Massoni, the Prefect of Police, said he was notified at 12.40 and arrived at 12.50. So he was much quicker than Diana's SAMU ambulance which took 17 minutes from notification.

They were not there on their own. The crash scene was actually a hive of activity, or inactivity, depending on how you look at it.

All up there were over 50 people who attended the crash site in an official capacity. That's over and above paparazzi, witnesses and public bystanders.

The earliest investigation – before the Brigade Criminelle took over – was carried out by three officers from the BCA. They were allowed to complete the initial plan of the Alma Tunnel crash scene.

It's amazing that these BCA investigators did not have torches and were forced to rely on the headlights of vehicles and the dull lighting inside the tunnel. BCA investigator, Thierry Clotteaux, said later: "In the tunnel the lighting was not so great". His colleague, Hubert Pourceau, told the inquest: "Because it was night-time [the single tyre mark] was not very visible".

Brigade Criminelle commander, Jean-Claude Mulès, took control of the French police investigation. Although he had spent 23 years in the Brigade he had never once investigated a car crash. Despite this Mulès told the inquest under oath that "due to my experience ... the director of the judicial police asked me and appointed me" to the investigation.

When Mulès arrived on the scene, he started looking for crash-related debris from the comfort of his car. He later said: "What we do is what we call a scanning of all the road from the car in the one way and also in the opposite way of the tunnel, and I scanned all the parts of the road to find any type of debris".

By 4.55 a.m. the crashed Mercedes S280 was removed from the tunnel. Then about five minutes later the cleaning truck moved in and cleansed the tunnel – removing any remaining evidence from the crash scene in the process. Within the half hour, at 5.25 a.m., the Alma Tunnel was reopened to traffic travelling in both directions.

A *Newsweek* correspondent, Christopher Dickey, arrived at the tunnel at 7 a.m. and was very surprised to see it open so quickly. He later commented: "I was astonished. This was Diana. She was dead. This was a big thing. I was sure the police would close the tunnel for several days, but it was completely open at 7 a.m."

Then, inexplicably, 2½ hours later, at 8 a.m., the lanes where the crash had occurred were closed again to traffic and the cleaning truck re-entered the tunnel. The crash scene was thoroughly cleansed for the second time.

The lanes were all reopened to traffic at around 10 a.m.

Before the Alma Tunnel was cleansed, the French investigation had found debris relating to a second vehicle, indicating there was a collision between it and the Mercedes S280.

On September 1, the day following the crash, Georges Dauzonne phoned the Paris police. He and his wife Sabine had seen a white Fiat Uno zigzagging and disorientated as it exited the Alma Tunnel just after the crash. Dauzonne said the police responded: "It does not seem to be very relevant for us".

Nearly three weeks later, after identifying the fragments found, the police told the press they were looking for a white Fiat Uno. Dauzonne called again and this time the police took statements from both Georges and Sabine.

French police made various claims during their investigation regarding a massive search for the white Fiat Uno. On September 18 they told the press they were "prepared to interview the owner of every Fiat Uno in France to trace the missing driver". Then on November 5 it was reported that "French police plan to interview 40,000 owners of Fiat Unos". The police said: "The car owners, starting with those in the

Paris area, will be invited to come to a police station to account for their movements on 31 August".

Martine Monteil, the head of the Brigade Criminelle, told the British police in 2006: "Investigations were carried out in respect of approximately 113,000 [Fiat Uno] vehicles, 5,000 of which were examined, with checks on the owners. No effort was spared."

There is no evidence whatsoever that any investigation of this type ever occurred. Official interviews of only two Fiat Uno drivers were ever documented.

First, James Andanson – he was not found during a police search, but instead was located as part of the Al Fayed investigation. After finding Andanson's Fiat Uno, the Al Fayed investigators passed on the information to the French police.

Second was Le Van Thanh, a Vietnamese person who painted his white Fiat Uno red around the time of the crash. It is very likely he was dobbed in by someone who noticed the timing of the paint job.

As it turned out, James Andanson was driving his own Fiat Uno in the Alma Tunnel on the night of the crash. The fragments and paint matched his car. And the witness descriptions matched him, his dog that was in the back and the age of his vehicle.

Andanson sold his Uno to a Chateauroux dealership on 4 November 1997, just over two months after the crash. He later lied to French police, telling them the sale was in June 1997, three months before the crash.

Then around Christmas that year James Andanson told Frédéric, Françoise and Josephine Dard that he had been in the Alma Tunnel at the time of the crash. He told Frédéric Dard, who was a well-known French author, that he wanted to collaborate with him to put together a book about the events. Andanson said that he could produce photos of the final journey. It appears that Andanson may have been promised access to photos taken by the MI6 motorcycle agents on the night.

Andanson was forced to shelve his plans when a month later, in January 1998, he was tipped off that the French police were going to be interviewing him. Andanson had been promised a clear run, but the police were forced into this interview as a result of research conducted by Al Fayed investigators.

Later that year Frédéric Dard became seriously ill.

Within two and a half years both Dard and Andanson were dead.

Dard died on 6 June 2000 as a result of the illness, but the circumstances of Andanson's demise, just a month earlier on May 4, were quite different.

James Andanson was incinerated beyond recognition while sitting in his BMW in an area of secluded countryside, about 400 km south of his home. Christophe Pelat, a fireman who attended the scene, said that he saw bullet holes in Andanson's skull prior to its disintegration.

No gun was found at the scene.

On 26 May 1999 the right front door of the Mercedes S280 was destroyed in a fire. Then four years later a French judge ordered the destruction of the right front wing.

It is no coincidence that these were the only two pieces of the death car that contained paint residue from the white Fiat Uno. The remainder of the Mercedes was shipped over to the UK after the British investigation started in 2004.

The French police had tried to avoid interviewing James Andanson, driver of the Uno, but were forced to as a result of the simultaneous Al Fayed investigation.

The same cannot be said about the several motorbike riders seen by witnesses along the route and in the tunnel. The police – French and British – made no effort at all to seek out these people.

Instead they implied that the paparazzi were possibly guilty and rounded up and arrested them at 12.40 a.m., 17 minutes after the crash. This action enabled the SAMU medical team – who arrived at the same time, 12 40 – to carry out their work generally unfettered by media scrutiny.

It had been part of the MI6 plan all along that the paparazzi would be held jointly culpable with Henri Paul, the driver. In the end, there could be no case against the paparazzi – and they were all released without charge.

The difference between the paparazzi and Henri Paul was that they were alive and could defend themselves. Henri Paul was dead and completely at the mercy of a regime that had to find an acceptable scapegoat for one of the greatest crimes of the 20th century.

In the meantime the true assassins – the motorbike riders and the ambulance doctors – remain free.

Even after the 2008 inquest, which found unlawful killing on the part of "following vehicles", there has never been any attempt by the

FRENCH RESPONSE

French or British police to find and arrest the riders of the following motorbikes.

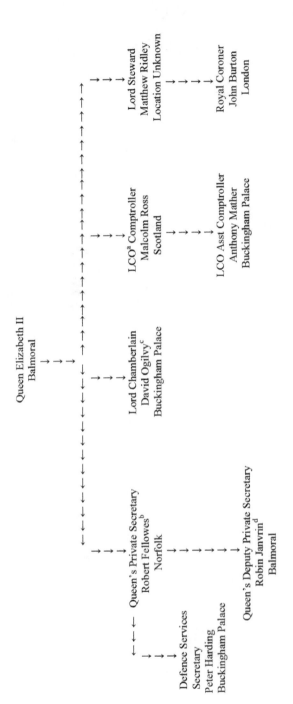

Queen Elizabeth II
Balmoral

Queen's Private Secretary
Robert Fellowes[b]
Norfolk

Defence Services
Secretary
Peter Harding
Buckingham Palace

Queen's Deputy Private Secretary
Robin Janvrin[d]
Balmoral

Lord Chamberlain
David Ogilvy[c]
Buckingham Palace

LCO[a] Comptroller
Malcolm Ross
Scotland

LCO Asst Comptroller
Anthony Mather
Buckingham Palace

Lord Steward
Matthew Ridley
Location Unknown

Royal Coroner
John Burton
London

[a] Lord Chamberlain's Office.
[b] Brother-in-law to Princess Diana.
[c] Earl of Airlie. Also known as Lord Airlie.
[d] Mary Francis was "Assistant Private Secretary" to the Queen at the time of the crash. Francis' location is not known, but she does not appear to have played a role in the events.

Figure 7

Diagram showing the British royal
power structure on 31 August 1997

16   Royal Control

Princess Diana's death was announced by the hospital at 4.10 a.m. local time – 3.10 in the UK.

Within minutes the phone rang at Lieutenant Colonel Malcolm Ross' home in Scotland. Balmoral – where the Queen was on holiday – was on the line.

Ross was the Lord Chamberlain's Office (LCO) Comptroller, directly answerable to the Queen. As a result of that call Ross picked up the phone and rang an old business contact, the president of Kenyons funeral directors in London. Kenyons had been the official royal undertakers until they were taken over by PFG[8], a French company, in 1991. Ross had worked with Kenyons during the late 1980s, when he was Assistant Comptroller in the LCO.

So when Ross was given the responsibility by the Queen to organise the embalming and repatriation of Diana's body from France, it was natural he would contact the head of Kenyons. He told the Kenyons president what was required – the full embalming by a female practitioner in the Paris hospital and the same-day repatriation back to the UK.

There was no time to waste.

At 4 a.m. (5.00 in France) the Kenyons president phoned Hervé Racine, the PFG president, who was at home in Paris.

These calls – initiated by the Queen – set events in motion on the Paris side. PFG was the leading funeral director in Paris and had the resources, even on a Sunday, to fulfil the royal directions.

---

[8] Pompes Funèbres Générales.

A same-day repatriation was very unusual, but the problem for the Queen was that Diana was no longer a royal – so the body of Diana was really outside of her jurisdiction. It was imperative for Balmoral to act so quickly that the events would have already occurred before anyone could start asking questions.

An embalming in France wouldn't be required with a same-day repatriation, but the Queen was keen to ensure there were to be no embarrassments. An early embalming would eliminate the risk of discovery of a possible pregnancy. Also, if Diana had been poisoned in the ambulance then evidence of that could be removed.

Blood and urine samples were to be taken during Dominique Lecomte's 5.30 a.m. autopsy – ahead of the embalming – and the results of those would be relayed via MI6 to Balmoral. It was important that those – along with the standard La Pitié Hospital blood test – were the only relevant tests and that knowledge of such samples being taken did not get out. That is why La Pitié has always denied taking a blood test on Diana, even though it is regular procedure in any hospital to do so. Records of samples taken were also omitted from the Mulès and Lecomte autopsy reports.

As an extra precaution, the samples taken later that day during the UK post-mortem were replaced by another dead female's. This was the royal order – there was to be no chance of embarrassment or scandal.

Back to early Sunday morning in Scotland.

This was to be a major cross-Channel operation and everything needed to work to precision. Malcolm Ross still had to make further early calls to get things moving on the UK side.

At 6 a.m. Ross telephoned his assistant in the LCO, Anthony Mather, who was at home in London. He ordered him to get down to Buckingham Palace and to organise a same-day repatriation.

Mather called the royal funeral directors, Levertons, from his home, before heading to the palace.

Every senior royal has a specific funeral plan, but because Diana had been removed from the family there was no plan for her. Mather told the police in 2005: "There was [not] a separate plan for the funeral arrangements of Diana, Princess of Wales, as she was not at the time of her death a member of the Royal Family."

Instead Ross told Mather during the 6 a.m. call to instigate Operation Overstudy, which was an RAF plan for the repatriation of royals who die overseas. But in addition he was told that there had to be an embalming of Diana in Paris before her return to the UK. Mather passed this on to Levertons, who organised two embalmers – with their equipment – as part of the team of three sent over to Paris. Their job was to embalm Diana and facilitate the UK side of the same-day repatriation.

This showed how important it was to Balmoral that the embalming be carried out in France. The French company, PFG, had been ordered via Kenyons to do the embalming. But as a precautionary measure, Levertons also had been told to make sure Diana was embalmed before bringing her back into the UK.

At 3.10 a.m. (4.10 in Paris) – the time of Diana's official death announcement – on 31 August 1997 the Queen welcomed the dead Princess Diana back into the royal fold, with open arms. Not only did she authorise the immediate use of Levertons, the royal undertakers, but she also ordered the use of the Royal Standard to be placed on the coffin inside the Paris hospital.

Then to further confirm this in the minds of the public, she despatched her son Charles to Paris to accompany Diana's body back to London.

There was no concern here for the interests of Diana. Charles was Diana's ex-husband. Less than two years earlier she had written a note, given to her butler, stating that she believed Charles was plotting her death in a car crash.

Charles was the last person Diana would have wanted accompanying her body back. But this was never about Diana's wishes. This was about the Queen's agenda to control Diana's dead body. This in turn allowed her to control the UK post-mortem and the samples taken and the later inquest. That was the primary objective.

To be able to bring that about the Queen had to bite her tongue and turn Diana back into a royal.

These actions helped enable the royal coroner, John Burton, to illegally take control of Diana's body as soon as it arrived back in the UK. The legal process was for the body of citizen Diana to be controlled by the coroner in the area of her anticipated burial, Althorp (as decided by the Spencer family) – that was the coroner for Northamptonshire.

It didn't concern the Queen that Diana wasn't buried on royal territory. Her sole short-term requirement was for control of the post-mortem and the samples. Anything after that, including the funeral arrangements, was of lesser consequence.

The Queen's 3.30 a.m. order for the French embalming of Diana was passed from Malcolm Ross, through Kenyons in London, to PFG in France.

At 7 a.m. – just six minutes before sunrise in Paris – Diana's body was moved into non-air-conditioned room 1.006 on the first floor of the hospital. Normal practice for dead bodies in hospitals is they are moved into the refrigerated morgue. Her body would be left to bake in that room for the next 5½ hours, deteriorating rapidly on what predictably became a hot summer's day.

Eventually that deterioration would be used as an excuse for the embalming. But the evidence is clear on two counts, that the embalming had been ordered from the early morning and the deterioration would not have occurred had the body been placed in the hospital morgue, or even in an air-conditioned room.

Colin Tebbutt, Diana's driver, entered the room at 11.30 a.m. He later said: "It was a hot day and in the room it was extremely hot."

The reality is that Diana's body was treated much worse than if she had been an ordinary citizen.

At 7.45 a.m. PFG called embalmer Jean Monceau of BJL, requesting a female practitioner to perform the embalming of Princess Diana at La Pitié Hospital. Monceau was told to liaise with Malcolm Ross in Scotland for additional specific instructions.

At 9.00 BJL made contact with one of their female embalmers, Huguette Amarger. Amarger, who was far less experienced than Monceau, wondered why she was chosen. She later told the police: "I learned that the British wanted it to be a woman to take care of giving the treatment".

Dry ice should have been applied to Diana's body, which was described by nurses as "melting", but it never was.

Monceau arrived at the hospital at 9.35. Amarger received further instructions at 9.45, but didn't arrive until 10.45.

Monceau still held off doing the embalming. He appeared to be waiting for the heat in Diana's room to increase to a point where those present would be clamouring for something to be done. But he also may have been expecting further instructions from the UK.

Monceau later said that he was trying to get authorisation. But the problem with that is the three people he says he got authorisation from have denied that. Martine Monteil, the head of the Brigade Criminelle: "I do not have any recollection of a conversation with Monsieur Monceau, the embalmer". Personnel from PFG have also denied speaking to him, as has Massoni, Prefect of police.

The reality is that the embalming was illegal. No documentation was completed. There was no authorisation and Diana's family were not consulted, as is required under French law.

At 12 noon, in response to media trying to get a vantage point for a view into the room, blankets were hung up in front of the windows. This increased the heat in the room even more.

It reached crisis point inside the hot room. At 12.15 p.m. Monceau spoke with the British Consul-General, Keith Moss, telling him about "the decomposition of the body and that the remains would be in a real mess" and he had been sent to "prepare the Princess's remains for viewing by the Royal party".

Then at 12.25 Prince Charles' police bodyguard, Peter Von-Heinz – who had flown across earlier in the morning – and an advance officer, entered Diana's room. They set about putting black sticky tape over the blinds to further prevent press intrusion. There is no way that the royals wanted the press getting any information about what was just about to occur – the Paris embalming of Princess Diana.

Amarger described it from her point of view: "Before I could start my work, I was put out by seeing the Scotland Yard police officers putting black sticky tape over the blinds lowered over the windows. There was therefore only a very little light and I was going to be hampered in my work."

Monceau may have been instructed to wait for Von-Heinz's arrival, because the embalming commenced at 12.30, immediately after they left the room.

The relatively inexperienced Huguette Amarger carried out the embalming under very difficult circumstances – hot conditions, poor lighting and she had Monceau telling her to hurry. Amarger said later: "There was a panic on. [Monceau] told me to be quick because Prince Charles was arriving in the afternoon".

Monceau forced Amarger to do the embalming even though there was no authorisation or documentation. This appears to be why he created the panic situation for her. He already had been told that Charles wasn't arriving until 5 p.m. – 4½ hours later – but did not pass that on to Amarger.

A normal embalming takes three hours but this one was completed by 1.30, in just one hour.

As a result of the pressure and conditions forced on the inexperienced Amarger, she did a very shoddy job. Robert Thompson, the mortuary manager involved in the later UK post-mortem, told police: "The Princess had been embalmed and it had been done particularly badly.... It seemed as though it had been done in a hurry".

There was only one part that had been done thoroughly and properly and that was the draining of the urine out of the bladder. No urine at all was left by the time the UK autopsy was carried out.

Diana's blood had largely been replaced as a result of emergency treatment in the hospital and the subsequent embalming. A test of the urine would have been the only reliable remaining way to establish pregnancy or poisoning.

One of the key reasons for the Paris embalming was to remove any possibility of a pregnancy or poisoning test. The complete removal of the urine achieved this.

Just as Huguette Amarger was commencing the embalming in Paris the Queen and other royals were arriving for the Sunday service at their local Crathie Church near Balmoral.

Despite Diana dying earlier that morning, it is incredible that the Queen instructed her name was not to be mentioned and no prayers were to be spoken in her remembrance. The minister instead gave his original prepared sermon about the joys of moving house, including jokes by Billy Connolly – even though Diana's grieving sons, William and Harry, were in attendance.

Earlier the Queen had told Charles that he would be required to travel to Paris later in the day to accompany the returning body.

Anthony Mather in London had been working towards that end – organising the transfer of an RAF BAe 146 from Northolt to Aberdeen. Malcolm Ross had made contact with Diana's sisters, Jane and Sarah, requesting that they join Charles. It was essential, from the Queen's viewpoint, that Charles was seen to arrive at the French hospital with representatives of Diana's family. This had to be viewed by the public as a joint mission.

Meanwhile the Leverton brothers, Keith and Clive, were in the midst of a real panic. They had to ensure they could get to the Paris hospital with two embalmers and equipment hours ahead of Charles. They were fully expecting to do the embalming before the repatriation and had not been informed of the separate instructions to the French companies, PFG and BJL. Clive Leverton told the inquest: "We had to get out to Paris quickly – we were under pressure getting our staff assembled". In 2004 he wrote in his police statement: "There were pressures and time constraints placed upon us". Mather had given them a 1 p.m. deadline to be on a specially prepared RAF flight leaving from Northolt.

At 11 a.m. the Royal Standard that was to be placed on the coffin arrived at Levertons, courtesy of the Lord Chamberlain, David Ogilvy.

They got the team together in time. Keith was to stay in London while Clive, joined by the two embalmers, David Green and Bill Fry, headed to RAF Northolt. Green had been camping on a farm in Dorset – Clive said later they had "a hell of a job to get hold of him".

The Leverton flight departed at 1.05. – complete with embalmers, equipment and the royal standard.

When they arrived at the French hospital at 3.40 p.m. (local time) they were greeted by the waiting French embalmers. To their relief, they were told that Diana had already been embalmed. Green later said that the French embalming was "insufficient for long term preservation".

The reality was that by the time the British embalmers arrived, neither Diana's blood nor urine was reliably testable for pregnancy or poisoning. That was all that was required ahead of the British post-mortem.

Meanwhile, the royal flight carrying Prince Charles left Aberdeen at 2.22 (3.22 in Paris), just 18 minutes before the embalmers arrived at the hospital. On route to Paris they would pick up Diana's two sisters, Jane Fellowes and Sarah McCorquodale.

The stage-managed royal production went very smoothly.

Footage and pictures went around the world of Charles, in unison with Sarah and Jane, rescuing the dead Diana from the French hospital.

The coffin carried out of the La Pitié Hospital was shrouded in the royal standard and accompanied by the royal undertakers. Then a choreographed 7 p.m. landing at RAF Northolt with media, along with the requisite welcoming delegation – Diana's private secretary and PM Tony Blair alongside royal officials, including the Queen's Lord Chamberlain.

Charles, Sarah and Jane disembarked.

Charles stayed around on the tarmac for 13 minutes before rushing back aboard, destination the more comfortable territory of Balmoral.

But Diana's sisters, Sarah and Jane, were furious.

They had learned on the flight back from Paris that the Spencer family would have no say in what was going to occur once Diana's coffin landed on UK territory. In fact, it was even worse than that – they hadn't been consulted regarding the Lecomte autopsy or the French embalming and had now been told by Charles that Diana was heading to Fulham Mortuary for a second autopsy, and then there would be another embalming. All under the control of the royal coroner and the royal undertakers. They even found out from Charles that there were plans to bury Diana in the grounds of Windsor Castle.

All this, even though Diana was not a royal and had been dumped by the Queen in 1996.

The two sisters, accompanied by Anthony Mather, decided to stay with the coffin and head to the mortuary where they would confront the royal coroner.

British royal coroner, John Burton, said that after hearing about Diana's death on Sunday morning, he called Buckingham Palace.

The truth is that Burton has been shown in the *Diana Inquest* series of books to have lied repeatedly in his evidence and it is quite likely – given the importance of his role – that he received an early call from Scotland.

Whichever way, Burton was told that there were plans to bury Diana in the grounds of Windsor Castle, she was being repatriated that day into RAF Northolt and Levertons were dealing with it.

The law in the UK is: "If a body is repatriated to this country it is generally accepted that the Coroner within whose jurisdiction the body will finally lay must be notified."

So jurisdiction falls to the coroner where the body will be buried.

The coroner who has jurisdiction determines whether there will be a post-mortem.

The Queen wanted the royal coroner to have jurisdiction, so that she could control the samples taken and the conduct of the UK post-mortem and inquest.

It had been determined by the Queen earlier on Sunday morning that Diana would be buried at Windsor Castle. In one swift stroke that solved the jurisdiction issue. Windsor Castle was royal territory therefore the royal coroner had jurisdiction. He would then control the post-mortem and inquest.

The problem though, was that the Queen did not have the right, legally or morally, to determine where Diana would be buried – simply because Diana was no longer a royal.

John Burton ignored that reality and proceeded throughout that day to make the arrangements for the post-mortem. He and his assistant, Harry Brown, organised the pathologist, Robert Chapman, booked the mortuary and dealt with Levertons and the police.

All of these arrangements were made with no attempt to consult with Diana's own family.

The first that anyone in Diana's true family learned about the royal coroner's post-mortem was when Charles informed Sarah and Jane on the royal flight. This would have probably been in answer to questions raised by them.

Sarah, Jane and Mather arrived at the Fulham Mortuary with Diana's body at 7.35 p.m. The sisters immediately sought an urgent meeting with John Burton. Mather later recounted: "I took them to the office area where Dr Burton spoke to them concerning his role and the post mortem examination."

Burton told the British police: "I ... explained to them that as the coroner of the Royal Household I had taken jurisdiction over Diana ... and was obliged to hold an inquest and order that a post mortem be carried out.... They left shortly after that. I believed at this time that Diana ... was to be buried at Windsor Castle, so I transferred jurisdiction from myself as coroner for the district of West London again to myself as coroner for the Royal Household in writing."

Burton was both royal coroner and coroner of West London, which included the Fulham mortuary. After the post-mortem he completed what is known as an s14 form to officially transfer jurisdiction to the royal coroner, himself. He says he did this because Diana was to be buried at Windsor Castle.

The problem with this is that during the meeting Sarah and Jane told Burton that Diana would be buried at Althorp. His notes made on 31 August 1997 read: "See family of Diana. Now to be funeral at Althorpe."

Burton knew Diana would be buried at Althorp, yet he went ahead and illegally controlled the post-mortem and illegally claimed jurisdiction over Diana's body as royal coroner.

Under British law the jurisdiction and post-mortem should have been under the control of the coroner for Northamptonshire, where Althorp lay.

After concluding the meeting with Sarah and Jane, at 8.20 John Burton walked through to the autopsy room and commenced the three hour post-mortem of Diana, Princess of Wales.

Then ten minutes later, at 8.30, Sarah and Jane slipped out of the Fulham mortuary accompanied by Paul Mellor.

A post-mortem was not required under British law – the Coroners Act 1988 states that it is at the discretion of the coroner. Diana had already undergone the Lecomte autopsy in France, yet the royal coroner, working on the Queen's behalf, went ahead and conducted a full three hour post-mortem.

A passenger in a car crash is not normally subjected to an autopsy – Diana was subjected to two within 24 hours of her death.

There were 11 men present in the room – the pathologist, the royal coroner, a doctor, the mortuary manager, two photographers and four British police officers. Nigel Munns, who worked as principal services officer at the mortuary, attended, but did not appear to have any reason to be there. Burton later told the police: "I am not certain what his official role was." Munns has never been officially interviewed.

Standard samples were taken – hair, blood, stomach contents, liver and eye fluid.

But when the samples were tested the next day by toxicologist, Susan Paterson, there was no sign of any embalming fluid or alcohol.

This was despite the fact that Diana had been embalmed in Paris and had been drinking alcohol throughout the evening before her death.

Paterson was confused by this because she had been made aware that the French embalming had taken place. She also knew that the femoral area, where the blood sample came from, was one of the embalming entry points listed by Monceau in France.

She carried out her own research, which included consulting with experts at the Royal London Hospital.

But she failed to resolve the inconsistency.

Diana was embalmed in Paris but now had no sign of embalming fluid in her post-mortem samples.

Fulham mortuary manager, Robert Thompson, assisted the pathologist, Robert Chapman, throughout the three hour post-mortem. He later stated in a sworn affidavit: "When her stomach was opened up there were signs of a recent meal and an extremely strong smell of alcohol". He told the police: "I was very surprised when I subsequently found out that no alcohol had been found in the Princess's body" samples.

There were other significant conflicts regarding Diana's samples – they have been documented in Part 4 of the *Diana Inquest* book series.

During the post-mortem the pathologist, Robert Chapman, took eight major organ samples from Diana's body that he failed to record in the post-mortem report. These were histology samples from the heart, brain, lungs, liver, kidney, spleen and adrenal, and an additional sample of the injured area of the heart.

The post-mortem concluded at 11.20 p.m. Thompson cleaned up afterwards and didn't leave the mortuary until 1 a.m. Burton told the police that he assisted with the cleaning but Thompson – who is a reliable witness – indicated he was alone during that time.

Chapman and the senior police officer, Jeffrey Rees, both failed to account for their movements at the conclusion of the post-mortem.

Somehow Susan Paterson, the toxicologist, ended up receiving samples that did not come from Diana's body, but belonged to another female.

The evidence – shown in detail in Part 4 of the book series – indicates that the samples were switched after the conclusion of the autopsy, at the same time as Thompson was cleaning up the autopsy room.

The royal coroner would have been working on instructions from the Queen. It is likely that this sample manipulation was carried out to completely remove any possibility of scandal or embarrassment arising from the results of Diana's post-mortem tests.

This is not something that the coroner could have done acting alone. It required knowledge of the internal workings of the mortuary, expert knowledge of how to manipulate body samples and labelling and support from the police in providing the extra required seals.

It is possible that John Burton, Jeffrey Rees, Nigel Munns and Robert Chapman collaborated on this in the "national interest". It did not involve a full sample switch – it was a sample manipulation. The samples of the other female would have been divided up – part used to obtain her results and part to obtain Diana's.

Diana's samples did not go to Susan Paterson at the Imperial College – instead she received and tested samples from the other female. The samples tested by Paterson were never subjected to DNA testing.

The police property register, completed at the time, reveals that Diana's true samples were "retained by Dr Chapman" and there is no record of them going to the toxicologist.

Whilst the tested samples have never moved from the Imperial College, there is a separate 2006 record of Diana's actual samples being at that stage in the custody of Operation Paget, the official police investigation into the crash, and LGC Forensics.

At 11.40 p.m. Diana's body was moved by Levertons from the Fulham mortuary to St James' Palace.

Keith Leverton later told the police: After the post-mortem "I then learnt from Mather[9] that Diana ... was to be taken to St James' ... as soon as possible.... I was aware that these [LCO] plans involved the requirement for embalming".

And so the second embalming of Diana commenced in the Chapel Royal at the palace, carried out by David Green, in the middle of the night. This embalming took 4½ hours and was completed at 4 a.m.

This was far from an ideal location to carry out an embalming, but that was not the Queen's concern. Her wish had been achieved – Diana was to spend her first night back in the UK on royal soil. In fact, very close to Charles' her ex-husband's official residence.

Clive Leverton was present during this final marathon embalming and has since said that "carrying it out at the chapel was not ideally

---

[9] Assistant Comptroller, Lord Chamberlain's Office.

suited". He told the inquest that "it was a very difficult situation, it was in the Chapel Royal".

St James' Palace lacked facilities for refrigeration or embalming – facilities that Fulham Mortuary had in abundance.

But the key is that Fulham Mortuary isn't royal property and the Chapel Royal is.

Diana had been subjected to the final indignity.

Within 25 hours of her death her body had endured a rushed repatriation accompanied by a person she suspected wanted to kill her, two post-mortems and two embalmings.

And finally was left to rest on royal property – an institution she thought she had been freed from.

PARIS-LONDON CONNECTION

17 Official Lies

As the dust settled in the Alma Tunnel, the official cover-up – in France and the UK – commenced.

The cover-up has been founded on a lengthy series of lies. These include lies that are exposed once they are subjected to even minimal scrutiny.

Late in the evening of 31 August 1997, British Ambassador to France, Michael Jay, wrote in his diary: "None of us here knew the Princess was in Paris and nor did the French authorities." He told the inquest: "I certainly remember, by the end of that day ... I was aware that the French were not aware of the visit". He also said: "I ... asked my staff to check with all the French authorities concerned to check that nobody was aware and I received assurances from them that nobody among the French authorities was aware of her presence."

Jay also told the police: "The Embassy was not aware that the Princess of Wales was in Paris until we were notified of the accident". And he told the inquest "nor was anyone in the Embassy" aware that Diana was in Paris.

Why was this issue of knowledge of Diana's visit so important to Ambassador Jay?

The reason is because if they had no knowledge that Diana was in Paris, then they couldn't be accused of involvement in her death.

Which is true.

It is effectively an alibi for the crash, but the problem is that the French and British claim that they were unaware Diana was in Paris is predicated on a lie.

There was a police car and two police motorbikes waiting for the arrival of Diana and Dodi's plane at the Le Bourget airport. Several witnesses, including the bodyguards and paparazzi, stated that French police escorted the party from the airport. Rene Delorm, Dodi's butler, later wrote: "We had a police escort until we hit the A1 autoroute".

So clearly the police not only knew Diana was in Paris before the crash, they even knew she was coming before she arrived. And not only that, they arranged an escort for her.

The plane arrived at 3.20 p.m. on Saturday afternoon, which was nine hours before the crash occurred. There was a group of paparazzi waiting at the airport and there is famous TV footage of the princess and Dodi stepping off the plane onto French soil.

There were around 40 diplomatic staff employed in the British embassy at the time, plus other service staff.

Jay expects us to believe that none of the 40 plus people in the embassy listened to the radio or watched the TV news that Saturday evening.

Included in Jay's embassy staff at that time were about ten MI6 officers. Their primary role is supposed to be gathering intelligence – so it is incomprehensible that they would be completely unaware of the presence of a famous British princess on their turf.

Jay's evidence indicates an unhealthy preoccupation with trying to prove that the French authorities and British embassy staff were unaware of Diana's presence. His diary entry appears to have him spending critical time on the very day of the crash, finding out who amongst the French and British were aware that Diana was in Paris.

In other evidence Jay claims that he had no knowledge Diana was being embalmed by the French in the hospital. He told the police in 2005: "I do not know at what stage I acquired this information [about Diana being embalmed], and I think that it was not until relatively recently."

This is despite the fact Jay made three visits to the hospital throughout the day.

This indicates the British ambassador showed more concern on the day about protecting the French and British authorities from anticipated speculation about involvement in the crash, than he did for the wellbeing of Princess Diana's body deteriorating in a hot room in the Paris hospital – and being subjected to an invasive and illegal French embalming.

The fact that Jay included this in his diary on the day of the deaths indicates that he had knowledge that this crash was no accident, and he needed to provide documentary evidence that could serve as an alibi.

Unfortunately it is a false alibi.

All the MI6 personnel in Paris have claimed that they were not working on the weekend of the crash – 30-31 August 1997.

The inquest heard that "Operation Paget took statements from all [Paris] SIS members". They said they were either out of Paris, or if they were in Paris they were off work and enjoying normal non-work-related activities like shopping, going to restaurants and holding barbecues.

Their evidence covered both days of the weekend – Saturday and Sunday.

An ex-head of MI6 France, Eugene Curley, stated during cross-examination at the inquest: "I am clear that [MI6] would have made arrangements for duty personnel, a duty officer and duty support staff". Curley, who was replaced as head not long before the crash, was talking about the arrangements over the weekend of the crash.

It is common sense that MI6, in a large strategic city like Paris, would have staff working in some capacity on the ground seven days a week, 24 hours a day. Their primary role should be gathering intelligence – they are an intelligence agency – and intelligence does not suddenly close down at dusk or when the weekend arrives. Intelligence is a full-time business.

So when the weekend of Diana's death comes around it is completely illogical for anyone – particularly MI6 – to claim that all personnel went home for the weekend. Yet that is what MI6 is saying.

There are basically two options. Either MI6 were involved in orchestrating this crash or they weren't.

If they were involved, then they would have had personnel working on the ground on the Saturday before the crash.

If they weren't involved, then, in their role as the eyes and ears of Britain in Paris, they would have taken a very keen interest in how it was that a popular British princess had died in their territory and on their watch. They would have immediately, on that Sunday morning, called in personnel to establish, for their own peace of mind, exactly what had occurred in the Alma Tunnel at 12.23 that morning. And why did the French ambulance take nearly two hours to get their much beloved princess to the hospital.

So either way – involved or not – MI6 must have had people working that weekend.

Yet MI6 insist that no one was working for the whole weekend.

That is a lie.

During the inquest only two members of the royal inner-circle – household and family – gave evidence. They were Robert Fellowes, private secretary for the Queen, and Miles Hunt-Davis, private secretary for Prince Philip.

Both insisted, sworn under oath, the Way Ahead Group only discussed administrative matters like scheduling of royal visits and tours. Hunt-Davis said it was set up "really just to coordinate their programmes". Fellowes said: "It was brought together as a coordinating group so that the activities, public activities, of the core members of the Royal Family ... were as purposeful and effective as possible".

Common sense tells us something different. The Way Ahead Group is called that because it has been set up to assist in determining the way ahead for the royal family firm.

Fifteen years of media articles, from 1996 to 2011, based on information leaks from within the royal household, also reveal that the Way Ahead Group dealt with major issues facing the royal family, including policy, future direction, public image and handling of problems.

In 1998 *The Economist* said the Way Ahead Group was working on a campaign to "modernise the monarchy". In 1996 the *Washington Post* wrote that they had been "discussing issues such as the succession and royal marriages to Catholics". *The Spectator* said the Way Ahead Group was making "an effort to chart the future of the Royal Family". *The Independent* wrote in 1998 that "the Way Ahead Group summit ... [meets] to consider long-term issues" facing the royal family. In 2000 *The Guardian* talked about "the efforts of Buckingham Palace's 'Way Ahead Group' to try to reinvent and modernise the monarchy for the 21st century". The *Daily Mail* said in 2006 the Way Ahead Group "makes the decisions which have shaped the Royal Family for the past decade or so". In 2011 *Vanity Fair* wrote "the Way Ahead Group ... deals only with ... paramount issues" facing the royal family.

And in July 1997 the *Sunday Mirror* said: "Top of the agenda at the forthcoming [Way Ahead Group] meeting is Diana."

It is evident that the Way Ahead Group deals with issues far weightier than the coordination of royal schedules.

When the royal private secretaries fronted up to the inquest, they could have stated that the Way Ahead Group addresses major issues facing the royal family. They could have added that Princess Diana was discussed in meetings, because she was a major issue facing the family at that time. That would have been the truth and no one would have questioned that – because it is common sense and fits with the evidence already in the public domain. The public would have expected that.

But they didn't.

And that indicates that they – or their principals, the Queen and Philip – have something to hide that they didn't want the inquest into the deaths of Princess Diana and Dodi Fayed to find out.

When Robert Fellowes and Miles Hunt-Davis stated under sworn oath that the Way Ahead Group deals only with coordination of royal schedules, they committed perjury in the Royal Courts of Justice.

Ex-British prime minister, Tony Blair, wrote in his 2010 memoirs about his final meeting in July 1997 with Diana at Chequers. He said: "Diana and I had a walk in the grounds.... I broached the subject of her and Dodi straight out. She didn't like it and I could feel the wilful side of her bridling. However she didn't refuse to talk about it, so we did, and also what she might do. Although the conversation had been uncomfortable at points, by the end it was warm and friendly. I tried my hardest to show that I would be a true friend to her, and she would treat the frankness in that spirit.... It was the last time I saw her."

Blair's description of this conversation with Diana relates to a meeting between them that took place on July 6. There was only the one Diana-Blair meeting during this period and the date is very definite – even though Blair actually leaves the specific date out of his book, saying only that it occurred in July.

The problem with this is that Blair describes himself warning Diana about Dodi, but Diana didn't meet Dodi until July 14 – eight days later – at St Tropez.

This therefore means that Blair has fabricated his warning to Diana about Dodi.

One could ask why Blair would go to the trouble of concocting this lie.

He goes on in his book: "I felt ... that Dodi Fayed was a problem. This was not for the obvious reasons, which would have made some frown on him; his nationality, religion or background didn't matter a hoot to me. I had never met him, so at one level it was unfair to feel nervous about him, and for all I know he was a good son and a nice guy; so if you ask me, well, spit it out, what was wrong, I couldn't frankly say, but I felt uneasy and I knew some of her close friends – people who really loved her – felt the same way...."

In relation to Dodi, Blair uses words such as "problem", "frown", "nervous" and "uneasy". And the context in his memoir in which he says this is around the Paris crash.

There could be an implication to the reader that the reason Diana is dead is Dodi Fayed. And not only that, but "I warned her off him" and "if only she had taken my advice Diana would be alive today".

The evidence around the case indicates that Blair did have a role in Diana's death. This falsified section of Blair's book appears to be an attempt to distance himself from involvement in the eyes of the public.

But his argument is based on lies.

Blair says he warned Diana about Dodi at their final meeting. But the meeting took place eight days before Diana had even met Dodi.

There are hundreds of official lies surrounding the case of the deaths of Princess Diana and Dodi Fayed. Included in this chapter have been just a few of the more obvious ones. The rest are outlined in the extensive *Diana Inquest* series of books.

But, why the lies?

They are part of a huge cover-up.

Why is there a cover-up if there is nothing to cover up?

18 British Response

Outside of the intelligence agencies very few in the British government had prior knowledge of the Paris crash.

Possibly only Tony Blair. Possibly his press secretary, Alistair Campbell.

The Commissioner of police, Paul Condon, does not appear to have been informed of British involvement until after the crash had occurred.

After he was notified, probably by MI6 Chief David Spedding, Condon called his Assistant Commissioner of Specialist Operations, David Veness.

The most popular princess in the world had just been murdered by her own government – Her Majesty's Government.

It immediately would have dawned on Condon that there would have to be a huge orchestrated cover-up operation, for the British police to be able to get through unscathed. They would be subject to pressure from the Establishment on one side and the public on the other.

The Establishment expecting a full cover-up operation and the general public seeking the truth of what occurred.

Scotland Yard would have to create a perception that the deaths were being fully investigated, when actually what was to occur was possibly the biggest cover-up the British police had ever been involved in.

This is not to say that individual officers on the case were aware that they were involved in a cover-up. There is actually a lot of evidence showing that particular British police officers were attempting to seek the truth of what occurred. Most of the corruption took place in the upper echelons of the investigation.

The first item of business on that Sunday morning was for Condon to appoint a senior investigator to head the British investigation. He couldn't just choose anyone – this officer had to be either someone he knew to be corrupt or someone he felt could be corrupted in the "national interest".

He would have sought the assistance of Veness in making that decision.

Realising the nature of the investigation required, it was quickly decided between Condon and Veness that it would be run by the Organised Crime Group (OCG). Within the OCG there were at that time four major investigation teams, all headed by Senior Investigating Officers (SIOs).

Three of the SIOs are known – Jeffrey Rees, Peter Heard and Geoffrey Hunt. The fourth name has never been revealed.

Peter Heard was travelling to Canada on September 2 – two days after the crash – so it was known that he was not available.

Geoffrey Hunt, who spoke French, was in London and was available and it is likely that the fourth unnamed SIO was also available.

Jeffrey Rees was already in the middle of an investigation into an allegation against Mohamed Al Fayed and other Harrods staff regarding theft from a safety deposit box. So there was an obvious conflict of interest, given that Al Fayed's son had just died in the crash and the Mercedes was being driven by an employee of an Al Fayed company, the Ritz Hotel.

That weekend Rees was away up north in Rutland with his family.

And Rees couldn't speak French.

So there were three very good reasons not to choose Rees – conflict of interest, the fact he was not available and didn't speak the language of the country where the crash occurred.

Yet Jeffrey Rees was chosen by Condon and Veness to head the investigation – ahead of at least one and probably two SIOs who were available in London on that Sunday.

On the afternoon of Sunday 31 August 1997, Veness arranged for a police helicopter to be despatched to Rutland to extricate Rees from his weekend away with his family, bringing him back to London to commence the investigation.

Jeffrey Rees did not disappoint his bosses – he dutifully fulfilled his role in the cover-up and committed perjury at the 2008 inquest, in the "national interest". His lies have been documented in the *Diana Inquest* series of books.

During a meeting at Kensington Palace on 30 October 1995, 22 months before she died, Princess Diana told her lawyer, Victor Mishcon, that she feared for her life. After the meeting Mishcon wrote up notes saying she had said that "efforts would be made if not to get rid of her (be it by some accident in her car such as pre-prepared brake failure or whatever) ... then at least to see that she was so injured or damaged as to be declared unbalanced".

Mishcon retained his notes from that meeting.

Two and a half weeks after the Paris crash, Mishcon contacted Scotland Yard and he met on September 18 with Condon and Veness, in Condon's office. Mishcon had the note with him and read its contents out loud, much of which has already been shown in Chapter 2 of this book.

Mishcon then passed the note to Condon and during or following the meeting Condon sealed the note in an envelope and locked it in his office safe.

When Condon retired in January 2000 he passed on possession of the Mishcon Note to his successor as police commissioner. John Stevens.

Six years after the crash, in October 2003, Diana's butler, Paul Burrell, went public with a copy of a separate note, but with similar content and this time in Diana's own handwriting. Diana had passed this note to him in October 1995. She had written: "My husband is planning 'an accident' in my car, brake failure and serious head injury".

As a result of the publication of the Burrell Note, Stevens and Veness decided to notify the royal coroner at that time, Michael Burgess, about the existence of the Mishcon Note.

Then in 2007, at the inquest, Condon, Stevens and Veness argued that it had been right to suppress the Mishcon Note because there was no other evidence that the Paris crash was suspicious. When Burrell went public they released it because there was now other independent evidence.

At the time the Mishcon Note was received by the police – 18 days after the crash – the French were conducting a full-scale investigation into the events.

Clearly the Condon-Stevens-Veness argument fails the common sense test.

It is common sense that if anyone – be it the police or anyone else – has evidence that indicates a death is suspicious and suppresses it, then they are guilty of the crime of withholding evidence from the investigation.

There is no question that if a person tells their lawyer – or anyone else – that they expect to be killed or severely injured in an orchestrated crash, and then that occurs, that is evidence relevant to the investigation.

This is not rocket science.

It is elementary information understandable to the average ten year old.

Condon, Stevens and Veness deliberately suppressed the Mishcon Note because they were an integral part of the orchestrated cover-up following the assassination of Princess Diana.

At the time of writing (June 2012) Condon, Stevens and Veness are subject to a separate French judicial investigation into their handling of the Mishcon Note.

19 Judicial Resistance

When John Burton, the royal coroner, illegally seized for himself jurisdiction over Diana's dead body, he effectively gained control for the Queen, his principal. This was control not only of the post-mortem conducted that night, but also of any future inquest.

It was clearly in the Queen's interests to acquire this control – it has since been shown that evidence points to royal involvement in the plan to assassinate Princess Diana. Control of the inquest would ensure the path taken would not be one that could uncover the full truth of what occurred.

UK law requires an inquest when a British citizen dies overseas.

Robert Thompson, Fulham Mortuary manager, stated in a 2001 affidavit: "I remember on one occasion Dr Burton walked into the [Fulham Mortuary] staff room whilst we were discussing Princess Diana and he said something along the lines of, 'I have a good mind to hold the bloody thing (i.e. the inquest) and not tell anyone'.... I am not sure why Dr Burton is continuing as Coroner in this case. He is aged 71 and the normal retiring age is 70.... As far as I know, he is solely staying on as Coroner for the Royal Household to conduct the inquest into Princess Diana. Unusually, he frequently carries the file relating to Princess Diana's post mortem with him. The usual practice is for the file to be kept in his office."

In April 2001, 3½ years after the crash, London's *Daily Telegraph* conducted an interview with John Burton. He told the paper that an inquest into Diana and Dodi's deaths would be "a waste of everyone's time and money. Nobody can be forced to give evidence as a witness and it would serve no purpose. The aim of an inquest is to identify the cause of death, but in this case all the evidence was collected in France and any inquest would just be a forum for different people's views."

The *Telegraph* wrote: "The coroner who is due to hold the inquest into the death of Diana, Princess of Wales is campaigning for a change in the law so that the inquiry never takes place.

"Dr John Burton, the coroner for the Royal Household, believes that any inquest into the Princess's death, and that of her companion, Dodi Fayed, would be costly and pointless. He told the *Telegraph* that he has been lobbying Jack Straw, the Home Secretary, for a change in the law that requires an inquest in every case where a body is returned to Britain after a death abroad."

This evidence indicates that John Burton had very little appetite to conduct an inquest into the deaths – even to the point of trying to have the law changed. And he also, aged 71, was hanging on to the role of royal coroner for as long as he could.

By March 2002, 11 months after the *Telegraph* article, Burton was forced to resign as royal coroner due to ill health. He died from prostate cancer on 8 December 2004.

Michael Burgess, Burton's deputy, took over as royal coroner, but he too failed to hold the required inquest.

But events did take over.

In October 2003 Paul Burrell, Diana's butler, published a handwritten copy of a note Diana wrote (quoted earlier) expressing fear of a plot to remove her in a car crash.

This was a circuit-breaker.

It led to the production by the police of the Mishcon Note and Burgess was forced to open the inquest in January 2004. At that point he called for the holding of a Scotland Yard investigation into the crash and John Stevens, police commissioner at that time, was appointed to head it.

Burgess then adjourned the inquest until the completion of the police investigation.

These happenings helped to further delay the inquest. The police inquiry, called Operation Paget, took nearly three years and produced its report, the Paget Report, in December 2006.

In the meantime Burgess had resigned as coroner of the case in July 2006, citing a heavy workload. He retained his role as royal coroner. It is likely that he actually resigned because it was becoming known that it was illegal for the inquest to be conducted by the royal coroner, because the royals had earlier taken illegal jurisdiction over Diana's body.

Elizabeth Butler-Sloss took over as coroner in September 2006 but she resigned just seven months later in April 2007, citing inexperience with juries – despite the fact that she had 50 years of experience in the British legal system.

It was becoming evident that the case was too-hot-to-handle. The inquest into the deaths of Princess Diana and Dodi Fayed was going to require a judge who was very corrupt.

Enter Lord Justice Scott Baker.

Baker took over as coroner for the case in June 2007 and he conducted the inquest, which commenced four months later, in October.

One of his first moves after becoming coroner was to remove Scotland Yard's Paget Report from the inquest website.

Then early in his Opening Remarks to the inquest jury on 2 October 2007 he stated: "The conclusions of the ... Paget Report are neither here nor there".

After all the toing and froing, including a three year MPS investigation that was deemed "neither here nor there", the British Establishment had effectively delayed the inquest by 10 years. It opened precisely 10 years 1 month and 2 days after the crash.

And by that time a substantial section of the British and worldwide public had "moved on" and had lost interest in the case.

PARIS-LONDON CONNECTION

20   Paget Pantomime

Operation Paget was one of the most flawed investigations in British police history.

John Stevens, who headed it, was already guilty of being party to the suppression of the Mishcon Note. Now, in January 2004, over six years after the events, he was entrusted with establishing the truth of what occurred in the Alma Tunnel on 31 August 1997.

Stevens was provided with the dossier from the two year French investigation, which had concluded nearly five years earlier, in 1999. In the end, after three years of investigating, Stevens parroted the French conclusion – Diana and Dodi died as a result of being passengers in a car driven by a drunk driver who was also speeding.

This conclusion was based on what were clearly two fraudulent autopsies on the Mercedes driver, Henri Paul.

The police ignored the evidence that revealed the fraud, ignored the clear evidence from the Ritz witnesses and CCTV footage that Henri Paul was sober and ignored the witness accounts of powerful motorbikes seen pursuing the Mercedes.

They also failed to interview hundreds of important witnesses that would have helped immensely in revealing a truer picture of what occurred. These included witnesses in the tunnel, witnesses near the tunnel, witnesses along the route, witnesses regarding the white Fiat Uno, paparazzi, key MI6 personnel in London, key royals in the family and household, ambulance personnel, Ritz Hotel witnesses, important French officials and police officers, witnesses regarding Henri Paul's activities, witnesses of the Henri Paul autopsies and witnesses of Diana's UK post-mortem.

Paget almost completely ignored the issue of Princess Diana's anti-landmine campaign, even though the evidence of the case clearly indicates that could have been a motive for her assassination.

There is really no area of the investigation that Operation Paget investigated thoroughly. And in the end the product of the investigation, the 832 page Paget Report, was deeply flawed and riddled with error.

The book *Cover-Up of a Royal Murder: Hundreds of Errors in the Paget Report* exposes the multitudinous flaws and deceptions in the report.

21 Judicial Corruption

After waiting ten long years, the conduct of the six month 2007-8 inquest into the deaths of Princess Diana and Dodi Fayed was really the final insult to anyone who was seeking justice in the case.

Lord Justice Scott Baker, who proved himself to be very corrupt, stopped at nothing in his efforts to manipulate the final outcome – the jury's verdict.

Baker did not act alone. He was assisted by the efforts of some of the lawyers present – at times, inquest lawyer, Ian Burnett, but more particularly those acting on behalf of the metropolitan police, Richard Horwell and Duncan MacLeod. Those two men lied repeatedly throughout the inquest, whenever they appeared to feel it was necessary to swing the jury's thinking towards their position.

Baker told the jury that the "conspiracy theories ... have been examined in the minutest detail through the evidence of over 250 witnesses". In total, 177 witnesses were cross-examined. But Baker failed to point out that there were over 250 other important witnesses who were not cross-examined. The jury needed to hear from a wide cross-section of witnesses to be able to form a properly balanced view of what occurred.

That never happened.

There were witnesses who have been shown in the *Diana Inquest* books to have committed perjury – sometimes repeatedly during their evidence – without any apparent accountability. These people include, in no particular order: Claude Roulet; Trevor Rees-Jones; Kez Wingfield; Paul Burrell; Alberto Repossi; David Meynell; Jean-Marc Martino; Arnaud Derossi; Robert Forrest; Véronique Dumestre-Toulet;

Jean-Claude Mulès; Jeffrey Rees; Jean Monceau; Eva Steiner; Clive Leverton; Michael Jay; Robert Fellowes; Anthony Mather; Robert Chapman; MI6 witnesses – Richard Dearlove, Miss X, Mr E Richard Fletcher, Mr 4 Eugene Curley; Lucia Flecha de Lima; Rosa Monckton; Keith Moss and Miles Hunt-Davis.

In addition to these issues, hundreds of critical documents were withheld from the jury's eyes and ears. These included very basic items like the post-mortem and toxicology reports relating to the bodies of the people whose deaths were being investigated – Princess Diana and Dodi Fayed. Hundreds of the most important documents – including those reports – have been reproduced in the book *Diana Inquest: The Documents the Jury Never Saw*.

Blame for withholding all this important information falls squarely in the lap of the corrupt judge, Lord Justice Scott Baker.

But he did even more to prevent his own inquest from arriving at a just conclusion.

Many key witness statements were taken by the French police in the hours, days and weeks following the Paris crash. The jury were not allowed to have access to most of those, but instead were expected to rely on a witness' recall in the stand of events that had occurred over ten years earlier. When the jury realised the importance of these statements, they made a special request to Scott Baker on 11 December 2007. Baker announced to the court that the jury had said that "they would like to be able to see witness statements". His reply to the jury was: "No, you cannot have the statements".

Baker had legal argument to support his decision, but it is clear that it neither passes the common sense nor the justice test.

There can be no comparison between a witness' account taken soon after an event and one taken ten years later.

This is very basic.

The jury were forced to arrive at a verdict, in one of the most important cases of the 20th century, with one hand tied behind their backs – only half of the witnesses were heard; much of the evidence that was heard relied on witness recall of events that occurred over ten years earlier; witnesses were allowed to lie under oath, often repeatedly, with no apparent expectation that they could be held to account; hundreds of evidential documents were withheld.

Then, as if to add insult to injury, Baker's 2½ days spent on his 80,000-word Summing Up was riddled with lies, omissions and manipulation of key areas of evidence. These instances – and there are many – have been covered in detail in the five volumes of the *Diana Inquest* series of books.

But there is more.

During his Summing Up, on 31 March 2008, Baker announced to the jury that he was withdrawing murder as a possible verdict. He told them: "It is not open to you to find that Diana and Dodi were unlawfully killed in a staged accident." Incredibly he added that "sufficient evidence [to support a murder finding] simply does not exist".

This meant that if they found for murder they would have to return an open verdict.

Clearly when a jury are told by a judge that murder is not an option, that then puts substantial pressure on them to return an alternative verdict – one that the judge has allowed and finds acceptable.

By the time the Summing Up was concluded and the jury commenced their deliberations, they had been provided with a substantially distorted view of what actually took place.

So it is really quite amazing that they were able to return a verdict that was different to what Baker was apparently hoping for. Baker may have been expecting a rubber-stamp of the French and British police conclusions – an accident caused by a drunk driver who was speeding.

The jury actually found that the deaths were brought about by "unlawful killing, grossly negligent driving of the following vehicles and of the Mercedes".

The driver of the Mercedes was known – that was Henri Paul. But the drivers of the "following vehicles" were unidentified – and were clearly not paparazzi, as has been mentioned earlier.

It is another major blot on the record of the British and French authorities that, since that verdict was announced on 7 April 2008, not a finger has been lifted in any attempt to establish the identities of the riders of the pursuing motorbikes. Given that they have already been found guilty by a jury of the unlawful killing of Princess Diana and Dodi Fayed, the next natural step would be to renew efforts to establish their identities.

Had the victims not been Princess Diana and Dodi Fayed, then that is what would have happened.

PARIS-LONDON CONNECTION

But instead, all we have heard since the conclusion of the British inquest is a deathly silence from the British authorities.

Why?

22 Conclusion

It is one of the most incredible stories of the century.

A young, aristocratic British princess – more British than the Queen herself – naïvely marries into the British monarchy. She is used and abused by her husband and others within that royal family.

She ends up finding herself living in a gilded cage, but with her every move analysed by an increasingly intrusive media – and an increasingly interested public.

In the end the pressure of the royal mistreatment and the public misperceptions becomes too much for her, so she decides she must tell the public her story.

This is unprecedented.

And that action is completely unacceptable to the Queen – it is unacceptable that a princess feels she can speak out about unpalatable royal truths.

The Queen retaliates by enforcing the royal separation. And it also, along with other issues, leads the Queen to set up the Way Ahead Group and announce her annus horribilus.

Then three years later the same princess speaks out again. This time, more forthright and more direct – on national television, at peak hour.

The Queen retaliates again. This time it is the royal divorce. And exclusion from the family.

But this lets the princess loose – out of the gilded cage she is enabled to fly free.

But too free.

The princess again upsets the Queen. And also leaders, presidents, prime ministers, arms manufacturers and dealers.

But this time the Queen has run out of legal options. She calls a special meeting of her Way Ahead Group.

A decision is made to remove the out of control princess.

The intelligence agency, MI6, is notified and told to do the job.

They talk to their friends in the US – they will help.

Then it is found she is travelling to France in two weeks' time. France says it will help.

The agencies work through scenarios and plan their moves. Some British people in France are not comfortable with doing the job. They are quickly transferred and replaced.

A car crash in the tunnel is decided on – it is very deniable.

The French, British and US have agents in all walks of life – hotel, medical, motorbikes and so on. Not everyone realises what they are involved in. Information is on a "need to know".

It comes together like clockwork.

But she survives the crash. The ambulance has already been set up as a back-up. The whole operation is very thorough.

She is effectively murdered in the ambulance. They take nearly two hours.

Then the hospital tries to save her.

They can't.

She's dead within six minutes of arriving.

The Queen acts quickly to control the body. The French act quickly to clean out the tunnel, twice. Destroying evidence.

The French conduct fraudulent autopsies. They quickly announce the results to the world. It is fraud.

The British act quickly to set up a corrupt investigation. And it does next to nothing for seven years.

The top Scotland Yard people suppress the princess' own evidence.

A corrupt French judge concludes it's an accident. After two years.

The British wait ... and wait ... and wait....

The butler goes public after six years. The princess' evidence is revealed. The public clamour for action. For the truth.

The British start an inquest. Then immediately adjourn it.

The police start their investigation. It takes three years. It's an accident.

It's corrupt.

CONCLUSION

Four coroners – Burton, Burgess, Butler-Sloss, Baker.

The Crown is finally ready.

But the people have had enough. They don't care anymore about the outcome. We want to move on.

For God's sake, let her rest in peace.

We don't want to drag the boys through this again.

The boys lost their mother. They want to know what happened.

Wouldn't you?

Justice Baker opens the inquest. Ten years late.

Six months of a mix of truth and lies. Six months of information and misinformation.

250 witnesses heard. Another 250 witnesses not heard.

The jury are confused.

Baker tells them: "Whatever your verdict ... it must be unanimous.... It must be the verdict of all 11 of you".

The jury deliberates.

Then, five days later, when it's not unanimous: "I am able to accept from you a verdict upon which at least nine of you are agreed."

It's 9 to 2.

The case is closed.

Justice has not been done. It probably cannot be achieved in the UK, France or US.

It may be possible in the International Court of Justice.

But as of 2012, 15 years after the tragedy, there is no justice in what has occurred.

In memory of

Diana

The Humanitarian Princess

When we lost her

We lost much more

Than can be imagined…

PARIS-LONDON CONNECTION

Maps, Diagrams & Photos

Bibliography

Books

Andersen, C., (1998). *The Day Diana Died.* New York: William Morrow & Co Inc.

Barnard, C., (2001), *50 Ways to a Healthy Heart*, Australia, Harper Collins

Blair, T., (2010), *A Journey: My Political Life*, USA, Alfred A. Knopf

Burrell, P., (2003), *A Royal Duty*, Australia: Penguin Books

Delorm, R., Fox, B., & Taylor, N. (1998). *Diana & Dodi: A Love Story.* Los Angeles, USA: Tallfellow Press.

Garner, Clare, House of Windsor Joins the PR Circus, *The Independent*, 23 February 1998

Holden, A., (1998), *Charles at Fifty*, Random House

Morgan, J., (2007), *Cover-Up of a Royal Murder: Hundreds of Errors in the Paget Report*, USA: Amazon

————, (2009), *Diana Inquest: The Untold Story*, USA, Amazon

————, (2009), *Diana Inquest: How & Why Did Diana Die?*, USA, Amazon

————, (2010), *Diana Inquest: The French Cover-Up*, UK, Lightning Source

————, Editor, (2010), *Diana Inquest: The Documents the Jury Never Saw*, UK, Lightning Source

————, (2011), *Diana Inquest: The British Cover-Up*, UK, Lightning Source

————, (2012), *Diana Inquest: Who Killed Princess Diana?*, Australia, Lightning Source

Morton, A., (1997), *Diana: Her True Story – In Her Own Words*, Australia: Harper Collins

————, (2004), *Diana: In Pursuit of Love*, Michael O'Mara Books

Sancton, T., & MacLeod, S. (1998). *Death of a Princess: An Investigation.* London, UK: Weidenfeld & Nicolson.

Simmons, S., (2005), *Diana: The Last Word*, London, Orion Books

Wharfe, K., with Jobson, R., (2002), *Diana: Closely Guarded Secret*, London, UK, Michael O'Mara Books Limited

Websites

Coroners Eastern District of London   www.walthamforest.gov.uk
Diana Conspiracy: www.dianaconspiracy.com
Famous Speech Transcripts   http://thespeechsite.com
Judiciary of England and Wales   www.judiciary.gov.uk
MPS Paget Report
     www.met.police.uk/news/operation_paget_report.htm
National Archives   http://yourarchives.nationalarchives.gov.uk
Official Inquest at National Archives
http://webarchive.nationalarchives.gov.uk/20090607230718/http:/ww
w.scottbaker-inquests.gov.uk/
Public Interest: www.public-interest.co.uk/diana
We The People   www.wethepeople.la

Media Websites

www.bbc.co.uk/news
Government Backs Diana in Landmines Row, BBC Politics 97, 25 June 1997

Newspapers & Periodicals

Alderson, Andrew, Coroner Seeks New Law to Forgo Diana Inquest, *Daily Telegraph*, April 1 2001

Allen, Peter & Arnold, Harry, Diana 1961-1997 – Investigation: Find the Fiat Uno, *The Mirror*, 18 September 1997

Buckley, Nick, Diana and, in the Aegean, Diana is Cruising Again, *Mail on Sunday*, 17 August 1997

Camilla's Car Flew at Me Like a Missile, *The Mirror*, 13 June 1997

Clinton Backs Diana on Mine Ban, *Daily Mail*, 19 August 1997

Collins, Laura, How Rupert Lost His Babykins to Big Willie, *Daily Mail*, 19 August 2006

Di and Dodi Crash Horror, *The People*, 31 August 1997

Diana Crusades Against Blasts from the Past, *Seattle Post-Intelligencer*, 17 January 1997

Duckworth, Lorna, "Diana, You Are Not Much of a Princess", *Mail on Sunday*, 16 June 1996

Evans, M., Diana's Life Could Have Been Saved Says Doctor, *Daily Express*, 19 June 2007

Fiat Uno Witnesses, *Hello! Magazine*, 17 January 1998

Golden, Andrew, Queen to Strip Harrods of Its Royal Crest, *Sunday Mirror*, 31 August 1997

Hitchen, Alexander, I Saw Fiat Driver Kill Di, *The People*, 18 January 2004

Kay, Richard, The Real Truth About Diana, *Daily Mail*, 29 November 2003

Kempster, Doug & Wingett, Fiona, Is Diana's Baby Clock Ticking?, *Sunday Mirror*, 20 July 1997

Klein, Edward, The Trouble with Andrew, *Vanity Fair*, August 2011

Lichfield, John, Car Search in Diana Inquiry, *The Independent*, 5 November 1997

Morrisroe, C., Diana's Last Secret: She Asked Me to Marry Her & Dodi, Says Priest, *The People*, 15 October 2000

Posner, G., Al Fayed's Rage, *Talk Magazine*, September 1999

Pritchard, Louise, A Harlot, a Trollop and a Whore...., *Mail on Sunday*, 10 November 2002

"This Is Diana Being Totally Irresponsible", *Sunday Mirror*, 13 July 1997

Revamping the Royals, *The Economist*, 12 March 1998

Robinson, Eugene, Elizabeth II Offers to Pay Taxes: Queen Trimming Family's Costs, *Washington Post*, 27 November 1992

Royal Family Gathers to Chart Its Future: Way Ahead Group Talks About Church Links, Rules for Succession, *The Spectator* (Toronto), 17 September 1996

Thomas, Gordon, Diana's Secret Tapes, *Canada Free Press*, 4 October 2006

Travis, Alan, Support for Royal Family Falls to New Low, *The Guardian*, 12 June 2000

Media Documentaries, Interviews and Transcripts

Channel 5, *Diana: The Night She Died*, Psychology News, 2003

Documents from Operation Paget Investigation File

Burton, John, Witness Statement, 16 June 2004

———, Witness Statement, 29 August 2004

Cole, Michael, Witness Statement, 6 July 2006

Derossi, Dr Arnaud, Witness Statement, 12 March 1998
Easton, Philip, Phone Call to Dr Pépin, 20 September 2005
Flecha de Lima, Lucia, Witness Statement, 1 September 2004
Gourmélon, Xavier, Witness Statement, 5 February 1998
Green, David, Witness Statement, 13 July 2004
————, Witness Statement, 17 September 2004
Jay, Michael, Witness Statement, 13 December 2005
Lecomte, Dominique, Forensic Report; Princess Diana, 31 August 1997
Lejay, Dr Marc, Witness Statement, 6 October 2005
Leverton, Clive, Witness Statement, 13 July 2004
Leverton, Keith, Witness Statement, 27 October 2004
Mailliez, Dr Frédéric, Witness Statement: 31 August 1997
Major Incident Property Register, Diana Princess of Wales
Martino, Dr Jean-Marc, Witness Statement, 12 March 1998
————, Witness Statement, 12 May 2005
Mather, Anthony, Witness Statement, 23 August 2005
Monteil, Martine. Witness Statement, 15 November 2006
Moss, Keith, Witness Statement, 22 October 2004
Mulès, Jean-Claude, Police Interview, 19 July 2006
Riou, Prof Bruno, Police Interview, 7 March 2006
Tebbutt, Colin, Witness Statement, 5 July 2004
Thompson, Robert, Witness Statement, 9 November 2004

Witness Affidavits

Chall, Trixi, Statutory Declaration, Beaulieu-Sur-Mer, France, 3 August 2011
Thompson, Robert, Affidavit, 13 June 2001

Author Information

John Morgan was born in Rotorua, New Zealand in 1957, and has lived in Australia for the last 24 years. He and his wife currently reside in Redcliffe, on the shores of Moreton Bay, near Brisbane.

John is an investigative writer with a diploma in journalism from the Australian College of Journalism. He completed his first book titled *Flying Free* in 2005 – about life inside a fundamentalist cult.

In his earlier life John was an accountant for various organisations in Auckland and Sydney. Later during the 1990s, he became a retailer operating a shop on Sydney's northern beaches. Since the 1980s John travelled widely throughout the Pacific, Asia and the Middle East.

He retired in 2003 at the age of 46, after being diagnosed with a severe neurological illness called multiple system atrophy. After a year or two of coming to terms with that devastating turn of events, he eventually found that the forced retirement created an opportunity to fulfil a lifelong ambition to write.

Following the death of Diana, Princess of Wales in 1997, John developed an interest in the events that had led to the Paris crash. Since 2005 he carried out extensive full-time research into those events and studied the official British police report after it was published in late 2006. John subsequently completed a book on that subject in September 2007 – it was titled *Cover-Up of a Royal Murder: Hundreds of Errors in the Paget Report*.

Throughout 2008 John Morgan continued his investigations into the crash and closely followed the British inquest into the deaths of Princess Diana and Dodi Fayed. That research resulted in the publishing of the initial volume of work on the inquest entitled *Diana Inquest: The Untold Story* – Part 1: *The Final Journey*. Six months later, during 2009, that work was followed up with the second volume *Diana Inquest: How & Why Did Diana Die?* The third volume, entitled *Diana Inquest: The French Cover-Up* was published early in 2010. It was followed by Part 4, published in 2011, entitled *Diana*

Inquest: The British Cover-Up. Then in 2012, Part 5, *Diana Inquest: Who Killed Princess Diana?*, was published.

This current short narrative book, *Paris-London Connection*, deals with the complete story of the Diana assassination and its aftermath. It is based on evidence gathered as a result of seven years spent investigating the Paris crash.

John can be contacted at: shining.bright@optusnet.com.au

Index

INDEX

INDEX

179

INDEX

181

INDEX

T

INDEX

CPSIA information can be obtained
at www.ICGtesting.com
Printed in the USA
BVHW071317270321
603571BV00007B/1375